13/02

79.

COLOUR
DICTIONARY
— OF —
HOUSE
PLANTS

MARSHALL CAVENDISH

This edition published in 1994 by
Marshall Cavendish Books, London

Copyright ©
Marshall Cavendish 1985-94

Editor: Susanne Mitchell
Art editor: Caroline Dewing
Designer: Sheila Volpe

ISBN 1 85435 724 7

British Library Cataloguing in
Publication Data:
A catalogue record for this book is
available from the British Library

Printed and bound in Malaysia

Contents

Introduction

This dictionary is intended to be more than a mere reference book of names, heights and dates. Within its pages you will find most of the genera (groups of plants) that you are likely to encounter in shops and garden centres.

Although it has not been possible to list all the species, let alone varieties, in a book this size, the general advice given for the most popular species will generally apply also to others. We have intentionally not given either heights or flowering times, because both are affected by varying conditions and thus are not easily predictable.

Throughout the book, dates are given as seasons, as months will vary from country to country. As a guide, the seasons are taken to mean the following in the northern and southern hemispheres respectively:

Early spring: March/September
Mid spring: April/October
Late spring: May/November
Early summer: June/December
Mid summer: July/January
Late summer: August/February
Early autumn: September/March
Mid autumn: October/April
Late autumn: November/May
Early winter: December/June
Mid winter: January/July
Late winter: February/August

Throughout the book we have tried to be realistic. If a plant has drawbacks we've said so. The methods of propagation suggested are those you can reasonably expect to succeed within the home: there may be other methods but these are not much help if they demand facilities that you do not have. If we have occasionally suggested throwing a plant away instead of trying to save it, it is because that is the road most likely to avoid disappointment—and even 'disposable' plants can give incredible pleasure and value for money if you regard them like long-lasting cut flowers.

Providing the right conditions

Tempting though it may be to buy a houseplant that takes your eye, you ought to know whether you have much chance of keeping it successfully. You may still want to buy it knowing that its life may be limited and be happy to accept that for the beauty it brings even for a short space of time, but at least you know what you can reasonably expect from it.

Three factors are most likely to influence how easy or difficult you wiill find a particular plant: how much *light* it receives, how much *warmth* there is and how much *humidity* you can give it. We have summarised these requirements as symbols for each entry:

FS Will tolerate full sun.
PS Needs a light position, but not exposed to intense direct summer sunshine between, say, 10 am and 4 pm
SH Will tolerate shade and should not be put in *direct* sunshine. Do not, however, expect these plants to thrive for long in a very dark position
HH Requires a very humid atmosphere to thrive. This may involve daily misting or the use of a humidifier
MH Less demanding but will still need a reasonable level of humidity, and perhaps misting or other measures to increase the moisture level in the air
LH Will tolerate a dry atmosphere
H Requires a winter night temperature of 18–24°C (65–75°F) to do well
W Should survive satisfactorily in a winter night temperature of 13–18°C (55–65°F)
C Will tolerate a winter night temperature of 7–13°C (44–55°F)

Brackets round a temperature symbol means the plant is not normally, or does not have to be, overwintered in the growing state (bulbs, corms and tubers that die down in winter, or annuals, for instance). You may be able to grow these satisfactorily even if you are unable to provide this temperature in winter, by adjusting sowing or planting times.

What the symbols mean in practice

We have simplified the requirements to take some of the mystique out of houseplant growing, and to dispel some of the myths. Precise temperatures sometimes given for houseplants can be misleading: where 68°F is suggested, no harm is going to come to the plant if the temperature drops to 67° or probably 65°; nor will it necessarily do much better at 70°. At a practical level, we simply do not control the temperature in our homes with the precision that a commercial grower might in his greenhouse. Many plants will stand lower temperatures than are often recommended if the compost is not too moist.

We have also given ranges for winter nights, because in the summer the temperature is what it is, and there is little most of us can do about it. And winter nights are when the temperature is likely to fall to its lowest.

On the whole, plants will tolerate a warmer range than indicated if the air is humid enough and watering is adjusted accordingly, but extra warmth is not always beneficial unless there is a corresponding increase in light to provide balanced growing conditions. And some plants actually *need* low temperatures. Most cacti will survive and grow if you keep your home at 27°C (80°F), but they are much more likely to flower if the temperature drops to 7°C (45°F) or even almost down to freezing in some cases.

Humidity is more difficult to adjust than temperature unless you use humidifiers. And lack of humidity is a major cause of houseplant failures. As a rule of thumb, those with the HH symbol are likely to be difficult to grow, and are perhaps best avoided if you are a beginner or do not have much time to devote to your houseplants. MH plants should be relatively easy to grow, but will still demand regular attention. LH plants are usually pretty tough, normally undemanding, and are likely to tolerate more neglect than the others.

A word on composts

Many houseplant enthusiasts advocate one type of compost rather than another—peat-based rather than loam-based for example. For the vast majority of houseplants both types will be suitable—what is more important is how you look after your plants. Peat-based composts are fine if you can keep the moisture level right, and feed regularly; loam-based might be better if you are less conscientious about watering and feeding. So we have given specific compost recommendations only where a particular compost has a more significant advantage—lime haters must have an acid compost for instance.

Getting the most from the book and your plants

If you choose suitable plants in the first place, and follow the cultural advice, you should get much more from your plants.

And if you are doubtful about a particular method of propagation, not sure of a term, or simply want to know the pros and cons of different types of feed, the second part of the book—Terms and techniques—should help.

The Plants

Achimenes
Hot water plant
PS/(W)/HH

There are about 50 species in the wild, natives of Central and South America, but today only modern hybrids are grown. There are varieties in shades of blue, purple, pink, yellow (uncommon), and white.

The Latin name is derived from the Greek *acheimenos*, the 'a' being a negative and *cheimon* meaning storm or wintry cold—in other words not liking cold. A cold spell during the growing season can give them a severe check and may cause them to go dormant. This characteristic probably helped to create the belief that they need watering with warm water, hence the common name of hot water plant.

Achimenes 'Early Arnold'

Although individual blooms are short-lived, they may continue from early summer until mid autumn.

How to grow
Achimenes prefer a greenhouse, but they can be grown successfully indoors with care. Good light is important, but direct sunlight will probably scorch the leaves. With too little light the plant will become leggy and flower buds will not form.

The plants die down for the winter. You can buy the dry rhizomes in late winter or early spring, or growing plants later.

Plant the rhizomes 10–20 mm (½–¾ in) deep in a lime-free compost and provide a temperature of about 18°C (65°F) to start them into growth. It actually does help to use water with the chill taken off to start them into growth.

Young shoots are weak and wiry so they may need support, or you can let them trail over the pot. To form a bushy plant, pinch out the tips of the young shoots.

Never let the compost dry out.

In autumn, gradually withhold water. When the stems begin to wither, cut them off and store the rhizomes in dry peat in a frost-free place.

Propagation
Divide the rhizomes when repotting, or take 5 cm (2 in) cuttings in late spring.

SOME POPULAR SPECIES	
The plants grown in the home are hybrids. Species are not used. There are,	however, named varieties that you can buy from specialist nurseries.

Adiantum
SH/W/HH

There are more than 200 species in nature, but less than about half a dozen are likely to be encountered as houseplants. There are, however, varieties of some species; some have minute leaves that give the plant a delicate, almost ephemeral look, while others have comparatively large, wavy and overlapping leaves that make altogether bolder plants.

How to grow
Most of the adiantums are far more successful in a warm greenhouse, than in the home. Unless you are prepared to use them as purely short-

term decorations, only consider them if you can give a warm position out of direct sun, and are able to provide high humidity *all the time.* Avoid cold draughts.

Use soft water and do not let the compost dry out. Use a lime-free compost when repotting.

Adiantum capillus-veneris

If by late autumn the plant looks the worse for wear, cut back the fronds, reduce the amount of water, but keep the pot in a warm place. After resting it for a couple of months, increase both water and warmth—with luck it will grow again.

Propagation
Divide the crown when repotting in spring. Spores are more difficult.

SOME POPULAR SPECIES	
A. capillus-veneris (Sub-tropical and temperate areas) (Maidenhair fern) Light green triangular fronds, black stalks. Seldom grows more than 30 cm (1 ft). There are several varieties. **A. raddianum** *(A. cuneatum)* (Brazil)	Less graceful than *A. capillus-veneris*, but more compact, and is less demanding than most adiantums. Young fronds are erect, but curve later. There are many varieties including the slightly fragrant 'Fragrantissimum'.

Aechmea
PS/W/MH

A group of bromeliads, most of which in their natural habitat grow as epiphytes. There are about 150 species in the tropical and sub-tropical jungles of Central and South America, but only a few are grown as commercial pot-plants.

Aechmea fasciata

They are usually bought in flower. Fortunately the flowers are long-lasting for the old plant then dies, to be taken over by offsets produced round base (these may take several years to flower).

How to grow
Keep the central 'vase' topped up with soft water during the growing season. On very hot days it is useful to spray the plant with tepid, soft water. Feed with half-strength liquid fertiliser poured into the vase once a fortnight during the growing period.

Propagation
Remove offsets when they are about half the size of the parent, and pot up in a compost of three parts ericaceous mix to one part sharp sand.

SOME POPULAR SPECIES	
A. chantinii (Brazil) Dark, olive-green leaves with pale, whitish banding. Flower plume has reddish bracts and yellow flowers. **A. fasciata** *(A. rhodocyanea)* (Brazil) (Urn plant, vase plant)	Funnel-shaped rosette of leaves up to 60 cm (2 ft) long, covered with silver-grey cross-banding. Pyramid-shaped, long-lasting, pink flower head holding tiny blue flowers. Some varieties have more grey on the leaves.

Agave
FS/C/LH

Succulent-like plants that develop a rosette of fleshy leaves, some of which end in sharp thorns. There are about 300 species, which grow naturally in the desert areas of America. Only the smaller species are useful as houseplants.

How to grow
Keep cool, but frost-free in winter. Can be stood outdoors during the summer. Water freely in summer, keep almost dry in winter. Feed once a fortnight during the growing season. Repot each spring, using a loam-based or cactus compost.

Propagation
Small plants sometimes form around the base—the quickest and simplest method of propagation is to detach these. Seed should germinate easily, but the plants are slow-growing.

SOME POPULAR SPECIES
A. filifera (Mexico) Makes a spherical rosette of stiff, upward-pointing leaves. Horny tissue on the upper surface and edges of the leaves breaks up to	form fine threads. **A. victoriae-reginae** (Mexico) Forms a globular rosette of dark green leaves edged with a thin white border.

Agave victoriae-reginae

Aglaonema
Chinese evergreen
PS/W/MH

About 50 species are known, most growing in humid, heavily shaded tropical forests of the Malay Archipelago, islands of the Indian and Pacific Oceans and China. A few species are grown as pot-plants for their variegated foliage. These plants have long been appreciated in the United States, but until recent years have been rather neglected in countries such as Britain. It is a pity, because they are quite easy plants and will tolerate a reasonable degree of shade if necessary.

Aglaonema commutatum 'Treubii'

How to grow

Best in a wide, shallow pot as there is not a big root system (a compost with sphagnum moss added will be beneficial).

Use soft water. Water freely during the growing period, but sparingly otherwise. Feed fortnightly during the summer.

The leaves of some species are damaged by heavy spraying, so use only a fine mist or take other measures to increase humidity.

Keep out of draughts.

Propagation

Dividing an established plant is the easiest method.

SOME POPULAR SPECIES	
A. commutatum (Malaya) Dark green leathery leaves, with silvery markings running out from the mid-rib. Varieties such as 'Pseudobracteatum' (longer, narrow leaves, paler green with white and yellow marks) and 'Treubii' (a smaller plant with more pointed leaves), are sometimes listed as distinct species. **A. costatum** (Malaysia)	Dark green leaves with white patches and white vein in centre. **A. crispum** *(A. roebelinii)* (Philippines) Large, pointed, oval leaves with dark green and silver streaks. **A. modestum** (Philippines) The leaves are plain green but it makes a plant up to 1 m (3 ft) high. Does well as a specimen plant when grown in a hydroculture pot.

Aloe

FS/C/LH

There are several hundred species, and though succulents they can form almost shrub-like plants. In a pot indoors the species grown usually make a compact rosette of fleshy, pointed leaves.

How to grow

Can be placed outdoors for the summer, where they will benefit from the sun. Keep cool but frost-free in winter (too much winter warm will inhibit flowering). Water very sparingly in winter. Feed once a fortnight during the growing season.

Use a loam-based or cactus compost when repotting.

Propagation

Remove and pot up offsets.

SOME POPULAR SPECIES	
A. arborescens (Natal, Cape Province, Malawi) An erect plant with thorny, curving, tentacle-like fleshy leaves. Spikes of orange-red flowers. **A. ferox** (Cape Province) The thick, fleshy leaves are covered with	brownish-red spines. 1 m (3 ft) spikes of scarlet flowers. **A. variegata** (South Africa) (Partridge breast) Upright rosette of banded leaves (dark green, V-banded white). Red flowers.

Aloe arborescens

Ananas
Pineapple
FS/W/MH

These bromeliads come from tropical and sub-tropical America, and include the commercial pineapple. The plants used in the home are, of course, grown for their decorative foliage and not the fruit, although a small fruit may sometimes form.

How to grow
Water generously during the summer, adding some water to the central vase formed by the leaves, and feed once a fortnight. Be careful not to overwater, and keep fairly dry during the winter. Mist with tepid water in very hot weather.

Small pineapple fruits may appear, but this brings that part of the plant to an end, and you will then have to grow on the offsets. Commercial growers can chemically induce fruits within about nine months of rooting, but in the home it may take several years for this to happen.

If repotting use a compost of three parts ericaceous mix to one part sharp sand.

Propagation
Remove and pot up offsets that form around the base of the old plant.

You can try growing a pineapple plant from the top of a fruit, though of course it will not make an attractive variegated houseplant unless you use one from a houseplant that has fruited.

Cut off the top with a tuft of leaves and a bit of the flesh. Remove the flesh, and leave the top to dry in the air for a day. When the cut surface has

Ananas comosus 'Variegatus'

dried out, plant the top in a free-draining, sandy compost. Cover the pot with a polythene bag to increase humidity, and keep in a warm, light place. Do not let the compost dry out, but avoid overwatering. With luck the top will root and grow into a plant.

SOME POPULAR SPECIES	
A. bracteatus 'Striatus' (Brazil) Green and cream striped leaves, which turn pink as a flower develops. Reddish-pink pineapple. **A. comosus 'Variegatus'** (Tropical America)	Sword-shaped, sharply-toothed leaves forming a rosette, with yellow bands along the length of each leaf. Typical small pineapple fruits.

Anthurium
Flamingo plant
PS/H/HH

There are about 500 species in the tropical rain forests of Central and South America, but only two are likely to be encountered as houseplants. The unusual 'flowers' are in fact a spathe (the leaf-like part) and a spadix (the tail-like part).

How to grow
These plants need care, and will not tolerate low winter temperatures, and during the summer they need high humidity. Use tepid, soft water for watering and misting. Do not over-feed. Be careful not to water too much in winter.

They are not easy plants to grow, but generally do well in a hydroculture pot.

Propagation

The easiest method is to remove rooted offsets from the old plant when repotting. You can take cuttings, but you will need a propagator to maintain humid conditions at about 27°C (80°F).

SOME POPULAR SPECIES	
A. andreanum (Colombia) (Painter's palette) The true species is not grown, as the hybrids make better pot-plants. The spathe (colours vary from red to white) is heart-shaped and the 'tail' straight. Heart-shaped leaves.	**A. scherzerianum** (Guatemala) (Flamingo flower) Only hybrids are grown now, not the true species. The leaves are lance-shaped, and the flowering 'tail' is curved. The brightly-coloured spathe is red or orange.

Anthurium scherzerianum

Aphelandra

Zebra plant

PS/W/HH

There are about 200 species in tropical and sub-tropical America, where they grow in jungles. They are not easy houseplants.

How to grow

Do not be disappointed if you can only keep the plant growing in a living-room and looking good for a couple of months.

The plants will usually be coming into flower when you buy them. Cut the flower off, together with one or two pairs of leaves, when it has finished, and rest the plant for a month or two. Repot in early spring, and increase moisture and warmth. Feed in spring and summer.

Many things can cause problems: the compost drying out, draughts, too much direct sun, too much shade, chills, and lack of adequate humidity (try to mist the plant at least every second day in summer).

Propagation

Stem cuttings can be taken from new shoots in spring. But you ideally need a propagator at about 27°C (80°F), and this is not an easy plant to propagate in the home.

SOME POPULAR SPECIES	
A. squarrosa (Brazil) (Zebra plant) This is the species usually grown, and the common name reflects the zebra-like pale stripes on the green, glossy leaves.	The 'flowers' (actually bracts) are yellow. There are several varieties, such as 'Louisiae' and 'Fritz Prinsler' (both particularly desirable).

Aphelandra squarrosa 'Louisiae'

Aporocactus
Rat's-tail cactus
FS/C/LH

The Latin name of this cactus is derived from the Greek word *aporos* (entangled). The cascading tail-like stems can look entangled. The common name of rat's-tail cactus is also indicative of the plant's habit: the round stems that cascade over

the edge of the pot look rather tail-like.

Flowers appear in spring.

How to grow
In nature these plants grow as epiphytes in rocky mountains at high altitudes. To encourage flowering, they must be kept cool in winter, but warmth (and if possible light) should be increased from late winter. Can be stood outside for the summer. Avoid turning the plant once flower buds have formed, otherwise they may drop.

Use a loam-based or cactus compost when repotting.

A very easy cactus for beginners.

Propagation
Cuttings rooted in summer will produce the quickest results, but can also be raised from seed.

SOME POPULAR SPECIES	
A. flagelliformis (Mexico) Green cascading stems sometimes over 60 cm (2 ft) long, covered with small thorns. Red flowers	7.5–10 cm (3–4 in) long. **A. flagriformis** (Brazil, Paraguay) A less popular species with stronger stems and violet petals and red bracts.

Aporocactus flagelliformis

Araucaria
Norfolk Island pine
PS/C/HH

In its native Norfolk Island (it grows elsewhere too), this plant makes a very large tree. Indoors it will make a fine specimen plant for a few years if you can give it the right conditions.

How to grow
This is a plant that has become increasingly difficult to grow with the more widespread use of central heating. It does not like a dry atmosphere. It is not an easy plant to keep in a modern living-room and will need frequent misting.

Araucaria heterophylla

Provide a well ventilated position (a north-facing window will suit it). Use tepid, soft water, giving hardly any in winter. Too much water in winter will cause the leaves to drop, as will compost that is allowed to dry out during the summer months.

Feed during the summer.

Do not repot too frequently otherwise it will become too large.

Propagation

Really a job for the professionals. Tip cuttings can sometimes be rooted, and commercially they are raised from seed, but both methods are difficult to succeed with in the home.

SOME POPULAR SPECIES	
A. heterophylla *(A. excelsa)* (Eastern Australia to New Caledonia)	Branches of needle-like leaves arranged in a graceful spiral.

Asparagus
Asparagus fern
PS/C/MH

A genus of about 300 species, most coming from East, West and South Africa. Although the fine, needle-like leaves of some species have earned these plants the common name 'fern', they actually belong to the lily family and are not ferns.

How to grow

Some of these species, especially *A. densiflorus (A. sprengeri)*, are tough plants that will tolerate either hot or cold positions. Water regularly from spring to autumn, only sparingly in winter. Feed once a week during growing season. Mist occasionally in hot weather or in a hot room in winter. Avoid too much shade.

Propagation

By division or by seed sown in spring.

SOME POPULAR SPECIES	
A. densiflorus (Natal) There are actually several forms of this plant and it is 'Sprengeri' (still widely known as *A. sprengeri*) that is the most popular. It has arching stems that will cascade if grown in a basket. 'Meyeri' has an erect habit with plume-like growth.	**A. setaceus** *(A. plumosus)* (South Africa) Very fine and delicate leaves give the upright but eventually arching shoots a feathery appearance. It needs a resting period in winter and is generally more demanding. There is also a more compact form called 'Nanus'.

Asparagus setaceus

Aspidistra
Cast iron plant
PS–SH/C/MH–LH

Aspidistra elatior

A genus of eight known species, only one of which is used as a houseplant. In the days before a much wider range of houseplants became really popular, this was one of the most common. It was a favourite not because it looks particularly attractive but because it is so tough. Nowadays it is quite an expensive houseplant to buy because propagation is slow by commercial standards.

How to grow
The plant will tolerate most conditions, but avoid direct sunlight, and do not let the compost become waterlogged. Although it will tolerate dry air, it is helpful to sponge over the leaves with clean water occasionally.

The plant will grow for several years without repotting, which it seems to dislike.

Propagation
Divide established plants in spring or summer.

SOME POPULAR SPECIES
A. elatior (China, Japan) Lance-shaped dark green leaves, often about 60 cm (2 ft) long, arising from the base. The purplish-flowers appear at soil level and though curious are not decorative. There is a more decorative variegated variety, 'Variegata', with irregular creamy-white stripes.

Asplenium
PS/W/HH

A large group of plants, ranging from hardy ferns suitable for the rock garden to tender tropical species often very different in appearance.

How to grow
The two species described below are visually very different. Neither is particularly easy unless you can provide the necessary warmth and humidity. Use soft water, watering freely during the summer (it is worth plunging the pot in water occasionally), and misting often. Keep plants out of draughts. Feed fortnightly during the growing season.

Asplenium nidus

Spleniums usually do well in peat-based composts.

A. nidus, being an epiphyte, can be grown on an epiphyte tree along with bromeliads (see Bromeliad tree, page 104).

A. bulbiferum looks more like a normal fern, but is interesting because small plantlets form on the surface of the fronds. These can be detached and grown on.

Propagation

A. bulbiferum is best propagated by detaching the small plantlets that form on mature fronds, but *A. nidus* will have to be grown from spores (this is not easy, and unless you are very keen it is best to buy plants, which are often sold as very young specimens).

SOME POPULAR SPECIES	
A. bulbiferum (Australia, New Zealand) (Mother fern/mother spleenwort) Foliage in feathery, arching sprays resembling large carrot tops. Small plantlets appear	on mature fronds. **A. nidus** (Tropical Asia) (Bird's nest fern) Pale green, glossy, spear-shaped leaves arising as a rosette. On a large specimen these may be 90 cm (3 ft) long.

Astrophytum

PS–FS/C/LH

A small genus of cacti with four species, having swollen stems divided into several ribbed sections. There are several varieties and hybrids. The funnel-shaped flowers usually occur in summer. These cacti are easy to grow once they are established.

How to grow

Always water sparingly—only when the compost dries out. Do not water during the winter, and avoid a humid atmosphere. They need to be kept cool in winter to stimulate flowering.

Repot each spring, using a loam-based or cactus compost, until a final pot size of 13 cm (5 in) is reached.

Propagation

These cacti are reluctant to produce sideshoots, which means that seed is the usual method of propagation.

However, progress is likely to be slow and cacti enthusiasts sometimes graft the young plants on to another genus to speed things along until the large astrophytum are enough to be grown back on their own roots.

You might be more tempted to buy a ready-grown plant rather than attempt to raise your own.

SOME POPULAR SPECIES	
A. myriostigma (Mexico) (Bishop's cap cactus) A globular plant becoming more cylindrical with age. Five or six prominent ribs give it a distinctive shape. The surface is often covered with scales.	Flowers yellow. **A. ornatum** (Mexico) A spherical to cylindrical cactus with eight ribs edged with clumps of spines. The surface has patches of white scales. Flowers yellow.

Astrophytum ornatum

Azalea

PS/C/MH

The botanical name for the main plant described here is *Rhododendron simsii*, but you will seldom see it labelled as this—usually it will simply be called azalea.

The name 'rhododendron' comes from the Greek words *rhodon* meaning rose and *dendron* meaning tree, and of course large rhododendrons do make trees covered with almost rose-like flowers.

The Indian azalea *(R. simsii*, once known as *Azalea indica)* is the plant most often sold, but sometimes the Japanese azalea *(R. obtusum)* is offered. It has fewer and smaller flowers, a disadvantage offset by the fact that you can plant it permanently in the garden once it has finished the indoor display.

How to grow
Plants are usually bought in flower, and if you buy with plenty of buds still to open you should have a long-lasting display if you keep the compost constantly moist (not waterlogged), and do not put the plant in a very warm room. Remove faded flowers regularly.

The difficulty comes in keeping the plant for another year. After flowering put the plant in a cool but frost-free room and keep moist with lime-free water. Once danger of frost has passed plunge the pot in the soil outside, and keep watered, fed, and misted regularly until early autumn. Bring into a cool room to flower.

If repotting (best done a month after flowering), always use a lime-free compost.

Azalea (*Rhododendron simsii*)

SOME POPULAR SPECIES	
R. obtusum (Japan) (Japanese azalea) Small, glossy evergreen leaves, paler beneath. Funnel-shaped flowers in groups of two to five. Various flower colours are available, as those sold are	hybrids. **R. simsii** (China) (Indian azalea) Masses of single or double flowers up to 5 cm (2 in) across. Small evergreen leaves. Those sold are hybrids and come in a range of colours.

Beaucarnea

FS/C/LH

The beaucarneas are interesting rather than pretty plants, but useful because they do not object if the compost becomes dry occasionally.

Although not well known in Britain, they are more popular in the United States, and in Los Angeles are even used as street trees.

How to grow
The plants can go outside on the patio for the summer, and need a light position while they are indoors. Water regularly once the compost begins to become dry in summer (and feed once a month), but water very sparingly in winter.

A loam-based compost will give the plant more stability.

Propagation
Seed is likely to be your best chance of success,

but it is not widely available, so you may find that you have to buy a plant raised commercially.

SOME POPULAR SPECIES	
B. recurvata *(Nolina recurvata)* (Mexico) (Pony tail plant) Long, narrow, arching leaves develop from a swollen base at first; a stem forms later. The leaves cascade	down, hence the common name of pony tail plant. **B. stricta** *(Nolina stricta)* (Mexico) Similar to the previous species, but the leaves have rougher margins.

Beaucarnea recurvata

Begonia
(flowering type)
PS/W/MH

Begonias form a huge genus, with more than 1,000 species, so it is not surprising that some of those used as houseplants are diverse in appearance and requirements. In this book, which can include less than a dozen species, they have been divided into two groups: flowering and non-flowering (which are on page 18).

The types most often used as flowering house-plants are the 'Gloire de Lorraine' and the Hiemalis/Elatior hybrids (of which the Rieger strain is outstanding because it is less vulnerable to mildew and bud-drop).

How to grow
Water freely when in flower, but avoid water-logged compost. Those listed below can be kept growing, but it is best to discard plants past their best and to propagate new ones.

Try to provide humidity, but avoid spraying the leaves directly as this may encourage mildew.

Propagation
Try taking stem cuttings, which may even root in water.

SOME POPULAR SPECIES	
B. elatior hybrids (Garden origin) Only hybrids are grown, and are sometimes listed as *B.* x *hiemalis*. These include the Rieger begonias. Mainly winter-flowering, but can commercially be made to bloom at other times. Many colours, mainly shades of red, pink, or yellow.	**B. semperflorens** (Brazil) Masses of small flowers over green or bronze leaves. Compact, mound-shaped plant. Many varieties are widely used for summer bedding, and they can be potted up and brought indoors to continue flowering during the winter.

Begonia elatior

Begonia
(foliage type)
PS/W/HH

There are over 1,000 begonia species (plus lots of hybrids and varieties), many of them with decorative leaves. The selection on this page includes the most popular types, but is only a small proportion of the many that you might encounter. Flowering begonias are on page 17.

How to grow
Foliage begonias need good light without direct sunshine, and a humid atmosphere (avoid wetting the leaves). During the warm months make sure the compost never dries out, but avoid waterlogging. Keep on dry side during winter. Repot each spring in a peat-based compost.

Propagation
Most foliage begonias can be propagated easily by leaf cuttings (the leaf blade should lie flat on the compost—see page 112), though you can also sometimes take stem cuttings.

SOME POPULAR SPECIES	
B. boweri (Mexico) (Eyelash begonia) Emerald green leaves with chocolate-brown marginal marks, edged with hairs. **B. masoniana** (S.E. Asia) (Iron cross) Green, corrugated leaves with a pattern of four or five bronze-purple marks.	**B. rex** (Assam) The original species is seldom grown. The B. rex hybrids have brilliantly coloured leaves in a whole range of colours and markings. It is difficult to keep a plant for more than a couple of years, but new ones are easy to propagate.

Begonia rex

Beloperone
Shrimp plant
FS–PS/W/MH

Although there are about 60 species of these tropical shrubs, only one—*B. guttata*—is grown as a pot-plant. It has been the victim of various name-changes and you might find it listed in some books as *Justicia brandegeana* or as *Drejerella guttata*. However, as it is usually sold as Beloperone, we have included it under that name.

How to grow
Water freely in summer, less in winter. Cut back straggly branches in early summer to maintain a good shape. Screen from too much direct sunlight in summer. Feed weekly from spring to autumn.

Beloperone guttata

Propagation
Take cuttings from young stems in spring or summer and root in a propagator.

SOME POPULAR SPECIES	
B. guttata (*Justicia brandegeana, Drejerella guttata*) (Mexico) Its common name, shrimp plant, reflects the shrimp-like appearance of the	clusters of petal-like bracts that overlap like roof tiles. The colour of these varies from brown to pink and yellow, depending on the plant.

Billbergia
PS/W/MH

Although there are about 60 species of these bromeliads in tropical jungles from Mexico to Brazil and Argentina, only two are widely grown as pot-plants.

How to grow
These are among the easiest bromeliads to grow. *B. nutans* is an almost indestructible houseplant, and will not come to much harm if the temperature drops below our suggested minimum.

The plants can go outside for the summer provided they are not put in a draughty position. Water freely in summer, but cautiously in winter. Feed every fortnight. There is no need to pour water into the 'vase'; watering the compost is adequate.

These bromeliads are best left to make large clumps, repotting only when the plant is tumbling over the sides of the pot.

Propagation
Divide an old plant when repotting, or if you want to produce more plants, pot up individual offsets.

SOME POPULAR SPECIES	
B. nutans (Brazil) (Angel's tears, queen's tears) Clumps of tall, thin, grass-like leaves, from which clusters of small blue, yellow and green	flowers cascade out of pink bracts. **B. x windii** (Garden hybrid) Similar to above species, but larger in all its parts.

Billbergia × windii

Blechnum
SH/W/MH

Although you may occasionally find other *Blechnum* species, the only one you are likely to find in garden centres is *B. gibbum.*

How to grow
This fern thrives in a shady position that is not too dark, and really needs to be treated as an isolated specimen to be at its best, rather than in a group of plants. Water generously from spring to autumn, moderately during the winter. Feed once a month during the summer.

Propagation
A large plant can be divided. Spores can be sown in spring, but this is not an easy method.

Blechnum gibbum

SOME POPULAR SPECIES	
B. gibbum (New Caledonia) Sturdy, light green,	leathery, arching fronds, radiating rosette-fashion and up to 1 m (3 ft) long.

Browallia
PS/(W)/MH

This genus of about half a dozen half-hardy annuals is represented mainly by *B. speciosa* and its hybrids. There are several named varieties, easily raised from seed, although they are better treated as greenhouse plants and just brought indoors to flower.

How to grow
Unless you have a greenhouse in which to raise your own, the plants are likely to be bought in flower. Simply place in a light position out of direct sun, water regularly and feed weekly. It is worth removing dead flowers as they occur.

Propagation
Seed, sown in spring or summer.

SOME POPULAR SPECIES
B. speciosa (Colombia) Trumpet-shaped, usually blue-violet, flowers, freely produced and borne above the lanceolate leaves.   There are varieties in various shades of blue, and also white.

Browallia speciosa

Caladium
Angel's wings
PS/H/HH

One of the most beautiful foliage plants with a very delicate appearance, but as it belongs in the jungles of Brazil and the Amazon it clearly needs a little coaxing to do well in the average living-room.

How to grow
The plants are grown from tubers, but you are most likely to buy a plant already started into growth. If the plant is to last any length of time indoors, you must mist it regularly (every day) and provide lots of humidity without getting the leaves too wet. Water freely during the summer,

Caladium × hortulanum

and feed once a week from mid summer.

By early autumn the leaves will have begun to shrivel and fall. Gradually withhold water, and keep the dormant tuber (in the pot) in a warm room for the winter. Repot the tuber 2.5 cm (1 in) deep in early spring and start it into growth at about 24°C (75°F) in a humid atmosphere.

Propagation
Tubers can be divided once they start into growth and you can see that each piece has an eye. Even so, you need to be able to provide very warm and humid conditions to be successful.

SOME POPULAR SPECIES	
C. x hortulanum (hybrids) These are derived from *C. bicolor* and other species. There are several named varieties. All have large,	arrowhead-shaped leaves on long stalks. Colours include white, cream, red, crimson, and green, many attractively blotched or veined.

Calathea

PS–FS/W/HH

A beautiful group of foliage plants, but unfortunately all rather difficult to maintain in the home. The leaves were used by the Indians for weaving baskets—the Greek word for basket is *kalathos*, from which the Latin name derives.

How to grow
The growing season is from early spring to early autumn, during which time the compost should be kept constantly moist (add a weak liquid feed once a fortnight). For the rest of the year, water cautiously—at no time should the compost either dry out or become waterlogged. High humidity is essential, and ordinary misting may not be enough.

Repot each spring, as the plants soon exhaust the compost.

Propagation
Divide an established plant in early summer.

SOME POPULAR SPECIES	
C. crocata (Brazil) Unlike most calatheas, this one is grown for its long-lasting orange inflorescence. Leaves are green with a reddish bloom. **C. lancifolia** *(C. insignis)* (Brazil) Long, lance-shaped leaves, up to 50 cm (20 in) long, purple beneath, green with darker alternating small and large	patches running off the mid-rib on the top surface. Perhaps the most attractive species. **C. makoyana** *(Maranta makoyana)* (Brazil) (Peacock plant) Leaves oblong in outline, about 15–20 cm (6–8 in) long, on long stalks. Silvery-grey with splashes of green radiating from the central vein on top, the pattern echoed beneath in purple.

Calathea makoyana

Campanula
Bellflower
FS–PS/C /MH

There are about 300 different campanulas in the world, from very hardy alpine species to half-hardy kinds that are really best as greenhouse plants. The two species described below make pretty short-term houseplants, but are not easy to keep from year-to-year indoors.

Campanula isophylla

How to grow
These plants need good light if they are not to become straggly, but avoid too much direct sunshine through a window. Both plants are best kept outdoors for the summer when not in flower. It is worth removing dead flowers.

Keep well watered during the summer, when you can also feed each week; water sparingly in winter. Mist occasionally. Repot each spring.

Propagation
Many campanulas can be grown from seed, but this is not an easy method indoors. It is better to divide a plant when repotting, or to take cuttings in spring.

SOME POPULAR SPECIES	
C. carpatica (Carpathian mountains) Cup-shaped, upward-facing blue flowers 25–40 mm (1–1½ in) wide, which completely hide the leaves when in full flower. Perfectly hardy,	and a useful rock plant. C. isophylla (Italy) (Italian bellflower, star of Bethlehem) A trailing plant with dull green stems and leaves and a profusion of star-shaped blue or white flowers.

Capsicum
Ornamental pepper
FS/C/MH

The ornamental pepper is a popular winter decoration. Although derived from *C. annuum*, the plants on sale are very much hybridised, which has given rise to fruits with a wide range of shapes and colours.

It is important not to confuse this plant with the winter cherry *(Solanum capsicastrum)* (see page 93), which also has berries in winter.

How to grow
Ornamental peppers are almost always discarded once the berries deteriorate and drop. Old plants seldom look attractive and new ones are cheap.

Keep in a light place out of draughts. Avoid a hot, dry atmosphere, and avoid overwatering (which may cause the berries to drop).

Capsicum annuum

Propagation
Seed sown in spring.

SOME POPULAR SPECIES	
C. annuum (Central and South America) (Ornamental pepper) The plants grown are hybrids derived from *C. annuum*. Grown for the decorative	berries, usually oblong and red, but many varieties, sometimes in shades of purple or yellow, and cone-shaped, fang-like, or round.

Catharanthus

FS/W/MH

You are quite likely to find the species described below (the only one cultivated as a houseplant) under its old name of *Vinca rosea*. It resembles a busy Lizzie (impatiens) in appearance, but is a more difficult houseplant to grow.

How to grow
Needs good light, but screen from intense direct sun. Mist the foliage periodically. The plant is best grown as an annual, and discarded after flowering. If you want to overwinter the plant it is best to take cuttings in the autumn.

Propagation
Sow in spring (they will be better in a greenhouse until they start flowering), or take stem cuttings if you want to try to overwinter the plants.

SOME POPULAR SPECIES	
C. roseus (*Vinca rosea*) (Madagascar) (Pink periwinkle) A misleading common name	for there are now white and white and red/pink varieties. Glossy green leaves with pale mid-rib.

Catharanthus roseus

Ceropegia

Hearts entangled
FS/C/LH

These creeping and trailing succulents (there are upright kinds too, but not used as houseplants) surprisingly belong to the same family as the stephanotis (page 95). They are interesting rather than beautiful.

How to grow
Water sparingly at all times, especially in winter. Feed fortnightly in summer. Ensure good light in winter.

Propagation
You have plenty of choice, so it is not worth bothering with seed indoors. You can try layering, division, or taking cuttings that include the small tubers that grow on the stem.

SOME POPULAR SPECIES	
C. woodii (South Africa) Long, cascading, thread-like stems with spaced out small heart-shaped mottled leaves in green and silver. Unusual-	shaped flowers (see illustration). Axil tubers form on the cascading stems and these can be used for propagation.

Ceropegia woodii

Chamaecereus
Peanut cactus
PS/C/LH

Chamaecereus silvestrii

This genus has only one species—*C. silvestrii*—although there are now hybrids involving other closely-related cacti.

How to grow
For successful results this cactus must be in good light, but not in strong direct sunlight. To flower properly it must be kept very cool in winter (a touch of frost will cause the plant to shrivel, but new shoots will form and the plant should flower prolifically).

Propagation
Shoots will often detach themselves, and these can be used as cuttings. In a greenhouse, seed is another practical method.

SOME POPULAR SPECIES	
C. silvestrii (Argentina) Finger-like, usually eight-ribbed, stems that tumble	across the surface and over the edge of the pot. Flowers easily.

Chamaedorea elegans
Parlour palm
PS/W/MH

Perhaps the most widely grown palm. It is easily raised commercially from seed, and usually marketed about 18 months later. Although growth is not slow by palm standards it is still slow in comparison with most houseplants, so you may find several plants in a pot to improve the appearance of a young specimen.

The plant may occasionally still be found labelled with its old name, *Neanthe bella*. In some places it may be found under the name *Collinia elegans*.

How to grow
Provide good light, out of direct sunlight, and water freely during the warm months, feeding occasionally. Water sparingly in winter, keeping the compost just moist.

Repot in spring if necessary.

SOME POPULAR SPECIES	
C. elegans *(Neanthe bella, Collinia elegans)* (Mexico, Guatemala) Arching, drooping pinnate leaves, with 12–15 leaflets on each side. Never grows	large (up to 1 m/3 ft), and even young plants will flower (the flowers look rather like yellow mimosa), and pea-sized fruits may follow.

Chlorophytum

Spider plant
FS–PS/C/MH–LH

Although there are hundreds of species, only two, in their variegated forms, are used as pot-plants.

How to grow
These tough plants will tolerate a lot of neglect, but will look that much better with some proper care. Water generously during warm weather, and feed every week during the summer. Occasional misting will be beneficial.

You will know it is time to repot when the thick, fleshy roots start to push the plant out of its pot.

Propagation
Simply remove and pot up young plants that form on arching stems produced by mature plants. Or layer them into pots to root first, then sever.

Chlorophytum comosum 'Variegatum'

SOME POPULAR SPECIES	
C. capense *(C. elatum)* (South Africa) Sometimes *C. comosum* is sold as this species, but they are distinct. In the variety 'Mediopictum' the long, linear leaves have a central cream band; in	'Variegata' the margins have the variegation. **C. comosum** (South Africa) The most widely-grown species in the variety 'Variegatum', which has a central white band.

Chrysanthemum
PS/C/MH

One of the most common flowering pot-plants, especially popular as a gift plant. Commercially they can be produced at any season of the year by adjusting the day length (using artificial light to lengthen the day, black curtains to shorten day-length). When you buy them they will have been dwarfed with growth-retardants.

In the home they should flower for several weeks if you buy them with plenty of buds still to open, but you will have to regard them as short-term houseplants. The effect of the dwarfing chemical will gradually wear off, and they will grow into tall, probably leggy plants, and if they flower again it will usually be in autumn. You could try planting them in the garden.

How to grow
Keep the pot in a cool room in good light (avoid direct sunlight in summer). Keep the compost moist, and remove faded blooms.

Propagation
Not suitable for the amateur. Although the cuttings are easy to root, the plants require special treatment afterwards.

SOME POPULAR SPECIES	
The modern pot chrysanthemums are derived from several	species, including *C. indicum* from China. There are many varieties.

Cineraria
PS/C/MH

Cineraria (*Senecio cruentus*)

This is one of those plants seldom sold under its correct name—*Senecio cruentus*—so it is included alphabetically under 'cineraria'.

There are many varieties: the biggest plants belong to the Stellata group, which can reach more than 60 cm (2 ft) high, and have thinner, more spiky petals; the Grandifloras have large flowers with broad petals and the plants are more compact, usually about 30–45 cm (1–1½ ft) high. The Nana type has smaller blooms but is compact and covered with flowers.

How to grow
Unless you have a greenhouse to raise your own plants, you will almost certainly buy the plant in flower. They are best discarded after flowering, but you can get the most from their flowering life by keeping them in a cool room, keeping the compost moist, and being alert for greenfly (to which cinerarias are unfortunately very vulnerable). Flowering will be shortened by temperatures over 15°C (60°F), too much sun, and too little water.

Propagation
Not a practical proposition indoors, but if you have a greenhouse they can be raised from seed sown in late spring or early summer.

SOME POPULAR SPECIES
Senecio cruentus *(S. cruenta)* (Canary Islands) Heads of daisy-like flowers, in many shades, some with contrasting zones, in winter or spring. A tender perennial grown as a greenhouse biennial.

Cissus
PS/W/MH–LH

The name of this genus comes from the Greek *kissos*, meaning ivy, which gives a clue to the nature of most species. The one most popular as a houseplant, *C. rhombifolia*, is known as the grape ivy. It is very likely to be sold under the name *Rhoicissus rhomboidea* and is dealt with on page 84.

How to grow
Water moderately at all times, and feed fortnightly while the plant is growing actively. Young plants will need repotting every spring. The climbing species will need a suitable support to climb up—simply bunched round a cane they

Cissus antarctica

lack elegance. Overgrown or straggly stems can be cut back in spring if necessary. The very beautiful *C. discolor* is a more difficult plant and will need more warmth and humidity—try standing it in an outer container packed with moist peat and keep it well away from draughts.

Propagation

Take stem cuttings about 2.5–5 cm (1–2 in) long in spring or summer. Use a propagator to help root them if you have one.

SOME POPULAR SPECIES	
C. antarctica (Australia) (Kangaroo vine) Climber with dark green, toothed leaves, about 10 cm (4 in) long. Not especially attractive, but tough and easy to grow. **C. discolor** (Java) A climber with heart-shaped, pointed leaves up to 15 cm (6 in) long	marbled silvery-grey, crimson beneath. The most spectacular of the species listed but also the most difficult. Needs warmth and considerable care: even then leaves are likely to drop in winter, and others may lose their colour.

Citrus

PS/C/MH

You can try growing most of the citrus fruits from seed, including lemons, oranges, and grapefruit. Most will make quite pleasant evergreens, although you cannot expect them to make long-term houseplants. And you really need a conservatory to have any hope of fruit. There is, however, a miniature orange, *C. microcarpa* (more often sold as *C. mitis*), that you may find sold as a houseplant.

How to grow

Never allow compost to dry out in summer. Feed from spring to autumn.

Propagation

Pips from citrus fruits should be sown on their sides and covered lightly with compost. Keep the compost warm and moist.

If you have a *C. microcarpa* plant that you want to propagate, try taking cuttings in spring. A rooting hormone and warm compost should help them to root.

SOME POPULAR SPECIES	
C. microcarpa *(C. mitis)* (Philippines) (Calamondin orange) Lance-shaped, dark green leaves. Small white,	fragrant, flowers and small oranges about 4 cm (1½ in) across, sometimes at the same time.

Citrus microcarpa

Clivia miniata
Kaffir lily
PS/C/MH

Clivias were named after Lady Clive, Duchess of Northumberland and governess to the British Queen Victoria. The species most widely grown, *C. miniata*, is a majestic plant.

How to grow
Water moderately from spring until autumn, very sparingly from mid autumn (only enough to keep the compost *just* moist). Keep the plant cool during the resting period.

A flower stalk should appear early in the year, but only increase the water supply and temperature once it is about 15 cm (6 in) long. If you do it too soon the plant will flower low down in the foliage. Once the flower has withered, cut the flower stalk off as low as possible.

Mist when new leaves or the flower stems are developing. Feed fortnightly from late winter to late summer.

Clivias dislike being moved around a lot, so try to keep them in the same place. They also resent root disturbance, so only repot when really necessary. Young plants will probably need repotting every year, but an older plant can just be topdressed by removing a little of the old compost from the top and replacing with fresh. If repotting, do it immediately after flowering, and be careful not to damage the fleshy roots. A loam-based compost is likely to suit them.

Propagation
New plants will form at the base of the parent. Once these have about four leaves and the parent plant has finished flowering, carefully remove them and pot them up. Do not divide the plant needlessly as a large clump looks impressive.

SOME POPULAR SPECIES	
C. miniata (Natal) Thick, strap-shaped evergreen leaves, arising in pairs that build up from the rootstock in layers.	Flower heads of about 10–20 orange or red blooms on a stiff, upright stem. There are several hybrids.

Clivia miniata

Cocos
PS/W/HH–MH

The species below is now more correctly *Microcoelum weddelianum*, but this palm is almost always sold under its older name of *Cocos*, hence its inclusion under that name here. It is unlikely to produce any coconuts.

How to grow
Use lime-free water. Keep the compost moist in summer. In winter, allow it almost to dry out between waterings.

Cocos weddelianum

Mist at least a couple of times a week with tepid soft water, daily if possible. Feed fortnightly in summer.

Repot in a loam-based, lime-free compost when necessary.

Propagation
Really a job for the professional growers, who usually grow it from fresh seed.

SOME POPULAR SPECIES	
Microcoelum weddelianum *(Cocos weddeliana, Syagrus weddeliana)* (South America)	(Dwarf coconut palm) A small palm. Needle-like leaves on fronds that will grow up to 1 m (3 ft) on a large plant. Eventually forms a small trunk.

Codiaeum
Croton
PS/W/HH–MH

There are about 14 or 15 species of codiaeum in the wild—mainly in Indonesia and Polynesia—but they are represented in cultivation as *C. variegatum pictum*. In fact so much hybridisation has occurred over the years that it is difficult to know what the particular parentage of a plant may be. Both leaf shape and leaf colouring are diverse, and the crotons are beautiful, but difficult, plants.

How to grow
If you want this plant to thrive in the home, make sure you can provide the necessary conditions: steady warmth, good humidity (be prepared to mist daily in warm weather), and freedom from draughts.

Good light is also necessary although plants should not be in bright sunshine. Keep the compost moist from spring to autumn, water more sparingly in winter but never allow the compost to dry out completely. Mist the foliage frequently to increase humidity. Feed fortnightly from spring to autumn and repot in spring when necessary. All of which sounds daunting but these beautiful plants are worth a little care.

If the plant is getting too tall, cut off the tip to encourage side shoots to form, or reduce the height by air layering.

Propagation
Not easy in the home. Cuttings can be taken in spring, and should root with the aid of a hormone rooting preparation and a propagator.

Codiaeum variegatum pictum

SOME POPULAR SPECIES	
C. variegatum pictum *(Codiaeum pictum)* (Malaysia) (Croton, Joseph's coat) Glossy, usually highly coloured and variegated leaves, forked or contorted	in some varieties. There are many varieties. Not easy long-term plants for the home as they need good warmth and humidity.

Coffea
Coffee plant
PS/W/HH

The coffee plant is an object of interest more than beauty, although its bright green evergreen leaves make a not unattractive shrubby plant. It does not normally flower and fruit until it is about three or four years old.

How to grow
Keep the compost moist (but not waterlogged) during the warm months, using soft water. Water cautiously in winter. Feed weekly and mist frequently during the summer. The plant should be rested and given less moisture from mid autumn to late winter. If the roots become too dry the leaves will curl up and dry out.

Propagation
Seed can be successful, but you will need a propagator or a warm place to germinate them in spring. Seed saved from your own pot-plants is not likely to grow. If you already have a plant, try taking cuttings; a hormone rooting aid and a propagator will help.

Top right *Coffea arabica*

SOME POPULAR SPECIES	
C. arabica (Abyssinia, Angola) Oval, dark green, glossy leaves. The small, star-like, fragrant white flowers do not occur until the	plant is about four years old and the green berries that follow them will eventually turn red. The form usually grown is a dwarf one, 'Nana'.

Coleus
Flame nettle
PS–FS/W/HH

If the coleus were expensive plants to buy they would perhaps be appreciated more. As it is they are inexpensive and among the most vividly and attractively coloured foliage plants that you can buy. They have been described as the poor man's croton (crotons are described on page 29). Sadly they are much less happy in the home than in a greenhouse.

How to grow
Coleus need as much light as possible, although

Coleus blumei

direct midday sun is likely to cause problems. The two most common causes of failure are watering with hard water or letting the compost dry out. Misting the leaves daily in the summer (occasionally in winter) will help. Feed weekly during the growing season.

You can overwinter coleus with care, but they usually become very leggy, and the leaves are likely to start dropping. It is better to start with fresh plants in the spring—they are easily raised from seed, or can be bought cheaply.

Pinch out the growing tips frequently to keep the plants bushy (one or two varieties are naturally self-branching: most are not). In the home, growth is likely to be uneven where the leaves grow towards the light. Give the plant a quarter turn each day to overcome this problem.

Propagation
Coleus are easily propagated from seed or cuttings. Cuttings are best if you want to over-winter plants, and especially if you want to save plants with particularly good markings. But overwintering coleus is not easy, and for the cost of a packet of seed you can raise more coleus plants than you can really hope to cope with. Sow in spring.

SOME POPULAR SPECIES	
C. blumei (Java) The plants grown are hybrids. The nettle-shaped leaves are very colourful, usually in	shades of red, yellow, green, and maroon. The blue or white flowers are insignificant and are better removed.

Columnea
PS/W/MH–HH

These spectacular plants really belong in the damp jungles of Central America, so not surprisingly they can be tricky as houseplants. But the spectacular bright orange, red, or yellow flowers of most species make it worth taking a little trouble with them. They are actually epiphytes, climbing, hanging or creeping in the jungle trees. In the home and greenhouse they are usually grown in hanging baskets—though the problem with baskets in the home is one of giving them enough light (it is usually poor near the top of a window).

How to grow
Water freely in summer, and mist regularly with tepid, soft water. Avoid wetting the leaves or flowers as they may become marked. Feed weekly during the growing period. Cut back the stems as soon as flowering has finished.

When repotting, use a compost of three parts ericaceous mix to one part sharp sand.

Propagation
Stem cuttings should root if taken in summer. A rooting hormone and warmth will help.

Columnea microphylla 'Grandiflora'

SOME POPULAR SPECIES	
C. x banksii (Garden origin) Cascading stems with small, glossy leaves, green above reddish beneath, and orange-red flowers about 7 cm (3 in) long. **C. gloriosa** (Costa Rica) Long, pendulous stems, pale to mid green leaves, and scarlet flowers, about 5 cm (2 in) long, with a	small yellow patch in the throat. There is a variety, 'Purpurea', with leaves flushed purple. **C. microphylla** (Costa Rica) Long, thin trailing stems with small, almost circular leaves covered with purple hairs. Orange-scarlet flowers up to 5 cm (2 in) long.

Cordyline
FS–PS/W/MH

Some cordylines, especially *C. terminalis* varieties, are popular if somewhat difficult foliage houseplants, but *C. australis* is altogether tougher and in mild districts is grown to tree size outdoors.

How to grow
Care depends on the species. *C. terminalis* needs the minimum temperature shown above, a position in good light but not direct sunlight, and regular misting. *C. australis* and *C. stricta* are tougher plants that can spend the summer outdoors, and will certainly tolerate lower temperatures if necessary. They will also tolerate direct sunlight, and have less need of frequent misting. Keep the compost moist during the warm months, just moist in winter.

Propagation
Offsets and cuttings are both practical methods of propagation.

SOME POPULAR SPECIES
C. australis *(Dracaena australis)* (Australia, New Zealand) A slow-growing palm-like plant with narrow, green, spiky leaves, about 1 m (3 ft) long. **C. fruticosa** *(C. terminalis, Dracaena*   *terminalis)* (South East Asia) Lance-shaped leaves, the varieties sold usually having red or yellow stripes. 'Red Edge' is a popular variety with narrower purple-bronze leaves edged red.

Cordyline terminalis

Crassula
FS/C/LH

This group of about 300 succulents is very diverse in shape and form, and some species make useful houseplants. The Latin word *crassus*, from which the name derives, means thick or solid, and it is the thick fleshy leaves that make crassulas a good choice for anyone who tends to forget to water regularly.

How to grow
These plants do not need a high temperature, and they will do well in a cool room in winter, and can spend the summer outdoors. Always water

Crassula arborescens

sparingly. Feed once a month during the summer.

Repot when necessary in spring using a peat-based compost to which some sharp sand has been added.

Propagation

Cuttings of shoot tips usually root readily, and many species will root as leaf cuttings.

SOME POPULAR SPECIES	
C. arborescens (Cape Province) Thick, sturdy stems, branching tree-like to give an almost bonsai appearance, but eventually making a large plant. Thick, fleshy, rounded to oval leaves, often tinged red at the edge. Established plants may produce heads of small white flowers.	**C. lycopodioides** (South Africa) Rather floppy stems completely covered with rows of overlapping scale-shaped leaves. **C. obliqua** *(C. argentea)* (South Africa) (Jade plant) Similar to *C. arborescens*, but flowers are pink, and the leaves rounder.

Crocus

FS–PS/C/MH

Crocuses are spring-flowering bulbs (actually they are corms not true bulbs) that need no introduction. Although commonly planted in pots in the autumn, they are not particularly easy to grow as houseplants.

How to grow

Plant six or eight corms in a flat bowl (or you can use a special crocus pot) in mid autumn. To force them, place in a cool, dark place, making sure the compost is moist but not wet (if the container has drainage holes ordinary compost is as good as bulb fibre).

Bring into the light in mid winter but keep them in a cool position. Put in their flowering position on the window-sill when a third of the flower bud is visible.

If brought into a heated room too soon, the flowers will not develop properly.

Propagation

Small corms will usually be found around the old one when you come to replant. Simply separate and allow these small corms to grow on for a few years until they reach flowering size. This is not something to do indoors of course and so is only possible if you have a garden.

SOME POPULAR SPECIES	
C. neapolitanus *(C. vernus)* (Mountains of Europe, particularly the Alps). The botanical name may not mean much; it is the	varieties derived from it— the so-called Dutch crocuses—that are grown: the well-known large-flowered garden crocuses.

Crocus 'Pickwick'

Crossandra
Firecracker flower
PS/W/HH

Crossandras are not easy houseplants, but they have become increasingly popular in recent

years. The flowers last a long time, but the plants can be difficult to keep because they require high humidity.

How to grow
Keep the compost moist at all times, but reduce the amount given in winter and make sure it is never waterlogged. Mist the leaves daily with tepid water and generally try to maintain a humid atmosphere. Feed once a week during the growing season. Remove dead flowers to prolong the flowering season. It is generally best to be realistic and throw the old plant away after flowering, raising new plants from cuttings (commercially these plants are raised from seed).

Propagation
Take cuttings in summer. Use a rooting hormone. Seed is likely to present problems in the home; you really need better light and facilities.

SOME POPULAR SPECIES	
C. infundibuliformis *(C. undulifolia)* (East Indies) Glossy green leaves about 8–10 cm (3–4 in) long,	acting as a foil to the salmon to orange-red flowers which are borne in clusters.

Crossandra infundibuliformis

Cryptanthus
Earth star
FS/W/MH

These bromeliads, often known as earth stars or starfish plants, are very easy houseplants. Most of the species have very attractively striped or banded leaves which form low, spreading rosettes.

How to grow
Good light is necessary for good coloration—some of them will be green in poor light, pinkish in bright light.

Water freely in summer, keep the compost just

Cryptanthus

moist in winter. Mist occasionally during the warm months, when you can also feed about once a month.

Cryptanthus have a small, shallow root system and do not need frequent repotting. They look best in a shallow container or growing on a bromeliad tree (see page 104).

Propagation
Small offsets form around the base of the parent plant. These can be detached and potted up but they will often detach themselves anyway if you wait.

SOME POPULAR SPECIES	
C. acaulis (Brazil) Makes a small rosette, about 7.5 cm (3 in) high. Various varieties, longitudinally striped. **C. beuckeri** (Brazil) Rosette of green leaves marbled white with a touch of pink. **C. bivittatus** (Brazil) Forms a rosette about 7.5 cm (3 in) high. Light	and dark green stripes, sometimes tinged pink. **C. bromelioides** (Brazil) Rosette-forming, but up to 30 cm (1 ft) high. 'Tricolor' has smaller leaves, striped cream, red, pink and green. **C. zonatus** (Brazil) Rosette of undulating leaves up to 20 cm (8 in) long, irregularly banded.

Ctenanthe
PS/W/HH

There are about 20 members of this genus in the wild, growing in the tropical rain forests of South America, mainly Brazil. They are unfortunately difficult plants to maintain in good condition in the home.

How to grow
Best grown among a group of other plants, where the humidity is likely to be better. Good light is necessary for the finest marking, but avoid direct sunlight. Use tepid, soft water, and be careful not to waterlog the compost. Water only when the compost starts to become dry. Feed once a fortnight throughout the growing season, and mist regularly all year.

Propagation
Divide large plants when repotting in spring.

SOME POPULAR SPECIES	
C. oppenheimiana *(Maranta oppenheimiana)* (Brazil) (Never-never plant) Lance-shaped leathery leaves about 38 cm (15 in) long and 10 cm (4 in) wide.	Dark green on the upper surface splashed with silvery bands and purple-red on the undersides of the leaves. The form 'Variegata' has brighter colouring.

Ctenanthe oppenheimiana

Cuphea ignea
Cigar plant
PS–FS/C/MH

There are about 250 species in North and South America, but only one is used as a houseplant. Its common name of cigar plant refers to the tubular red flowers that have a small grey, ash-like rim.

How to grow
The plant can be stood outside for the summer, but if in a window indoors provide some shade from the intense midday sun (otherwise the leaves may be damaged).

Water freely in summer, and feed once a week. Water only moderately in winter and do not feed. Misting should not be necessary.

Cut back straggly stems in spring to avoid legginess. However, it is better to raise new plants each year and to discard the old ones.

Propagation
Seed is a sensible method if you have a greenhouse; indoor cuttings are probably better. These can be taken in spring or autumn. Both cuttings and seedlings should have the growing tips pinched out several times to encourage bushiness.

SOME POPULAR SPECIES	
C. ignea (Mexico) Cigar-shaped red flowers with ash-grey tips set off	among a mass of mid green leaves up to 5 cm (2 in) long.

Cuphea ignea

Cycas
Sago palm
PS/W/MH

Cycas resemble palms, but botanically they are not. In fact they are very ancient plants that were already growing in the Carboniferous age, and they might well have formed the staple diet of the dinosaurs. Young plants are likely to be little more than 60 cm (2 ft) high with the arching fronds arising from a central core.

The common name of sago palm refers to the fact that the pith contains a starchy farina, but it

Cycas revoluta

has to be washed thoroughly to remove any traces of a poisonous substance also found in the plant before it can be used. And as the cycas grows only slowly anyway, it has never become an economic source of food.

How to grow
Although best in diffused daylight in summer, a position in full light is best in winter. Mist with tepid, soft water occasionally, and feed weekly in summer. Young plants will need repotting each spring, older ones just need topdressing.

Propagation
Not really a practical proposition in the home. You need a supply of fresh seed, and even with good conditions germination may take several months.

SOME POPULAR SPECIES	
C. revoluta (China) Forms a head of stiff, arching, palm-like but feathery fronds, little more	than 30 cm (1 ft) long on young plants, up to 1.8 m (6 ft) on old plants. Stem forms a rounded base.

Cyclamen
PS/C–W/MH

Cyclamen persicum

This instantly-recognisable genus has 15 species that grow wild in the Mediterranean countries and islands, and in Asia Minor and Iran. Some are hardy plants suitable for the rock garden, but those we grow as houseplants are derived from the tender *C. persicum*.

How to grow
Most cyclamen are bought in flower. To prolong the flowering period, avoid a very warm room, direct sun, and draughts. Remove faded flowers and yellowing leaves, and avoid over-watering (and try to keep the top of the corm dry when you are watering).

In order to attempt to keep the plant for another year, give less water after flowering, and stand the plant outside in a cool shady spot for summer. Repot the corm in a soil-based compost in late summer, start it into growth again by watering, and feed weekly until flower buds appear.

Propagation
Cyclamen are raised from seed, but for good results the plants are best grown in a greenhouse until coming into flower. Late summer or late winter are the usual sowing times. You will need a propagator, and even then germination may take a month or even longer.

SOME POPULAR SPECIES	
C. persicum (E. Mediterranean regions) Oval to heart-shaped leaves, usually attractively marbled, topped by	flowers with strongly reflexed petals. Some strains have ruffled or fringed petals, and there are miniatures.

Cyperus
Umbrella plant
PS–SH/W/MH

A genus of 550 rush-like, moisture-loving plants, and including the papyrus plant of biblical fame. Two species are commonly grown as house-plants—both of which are useful for anyone who tends to overwater houseplants.

How to grow
Happiest with its roots constantly in water, certainly the compost should not dry out. Feed weekly from mid spring to mid autumn. Repot each spring.

Propagation
The simplest way is to divide a plant when repotting. This method is quick and trouble-free.

SOME POPULAR SPECIES	
C. alternifolius (Africa) Forms a compact clump of rush-like stems 60–75 cm (2–2½ ft) tall, with green leaves arranged umbrella-fashion on the top.	**C. diffusus** (Australia) Similar to the last species but with wider leaves and does not grow more than about 50 cm (20 in) tall.

Cyperus alternifolius

Cyrtomium
Holly fern
PS–SH/W/MH

The species usually grown *(C. falcatum)* is a tough fern, much more able to tolerate a smoky atmosphere and draughts than most ferns. Un-typically for a fern, it has glossy, leathery leaves that actually look tough.

How to grow
Avoid a hot, dry position, and never let the compost dry out. Mist about twice a week in summer,

Cyrtomium falcatum

once in winter (although they will still grow with less humidity than most ferns). Feed weekly during the warm months, and repot each spring.

Propagation
Division is the simplest method. You could try raising them from spores, but it is not a quick or easy method even with good facilities.

SOME POPULAR SPECIES	
C. falcatum *(Polystichum falcatum)* (China, Japan, Himalayas) Deep green, glossy, pinnate fronds. The	pinnae are particularly large in the variety 'Rochfordianum'. A dependable and attractive houseplant.

Dieffenbachia
Dumb cane
PS/H/HH–MH

Some of the dieffenbachias are among the most popular houseplants, although they are not particularly easy to grow and are potentially hazardous. The common name dumb cane comes from the ability of the sap to cause such irritation to the throat, tongue and mouth, that victims have been unable to speak. More seriously there have been reported cases of life being threatened because respiration has been affected. Millions of these plants are grown in homes with no problems, however, so it is important to keep a sense of perspective. They are perhaps best avoided if there is a toddler or maybe a cat that could be tempted to chew the leaves. Otherwise, simply wash your hands after removing leaves or taking a cutting, and make sure the sap does not get into the mouth.

How to grow
From spring onwards water generously and mist regularly, using tepid, soft water for both. Feed weekly in summer. Water sparingly from mid autumn to late winter (but continue to mist occasionally). The leaves and appearance will benefit if the leaves are gently sprayed with lukewarm water occasionally. Repot annually.

Lower leaves are likely to fall with time. Even with careful watering and misting it is difficult to avoid this in the home.

Propagation
If the plant has become very leggy, try cutting back the stem to about 10 cm (4 in): daughter plants may form at the base that you can use as cuttings. Sections of the removed stem can be used as eye cuttings. If you only want to replace the old plant with a better-looking new one, try air layering.

SOME POPULAR SPECIES	
D. amoena (Tropical America) Oblong, dark green leaves, marbled white and cream along the side veins, up to 60 cm (2 ft) long in mature plants. The thick stem may become trunk-like. There are several varieties, such as 'Tropic Snow' (which has more pronounced white markings). **D. x bausei** (Garden origin) Yellowish-green leaves with splashes of dark green, and flecks of white.	**D. bowmannii** (Japan) A large-leaved species— up to 75 cm (2½ ft) long. The leaves are dull green with some white patches. There are varieties with more pronounced white variegation. **D. maculata** *(D. picta)* (Brazil, Colombia) Oblong leaves about 30 cm (1 ft) long, dark green splashed cream. There are several varieties, some with more pronounced cream or silver markings, others also with light and dark green patterns.

Dieffenbachia maculata

Dionaea

Venus fly trap

SH/C/HH

It is hard to imagine anyone growing the Venus fly trap as a decorative houseplant, but it is undoubtedly fascinating. Certainly it will catch the imagination of children with its ability to close its leaves to trap flies and then digesting them.

There is only the one species, and this grows wild in a rather local area of damp, mossy, marshy land near the coast of Carolina, USA. The chances of keeping the Venus fly trap for long in the home are not good.

How to grow

Water freely—the compost must never become dry, even in winter. To provide an atmosphere that is humid enough, try covering it with a glass dome, or something similar, or placing it close to a humidifier. Misting, even daily, will not really be adequate.

Do not feed the plant—it will get some of its nutrients from the insects that it catches.

If you repot, use a mixture of peat and sphagnum moss, together with a little soil.

Propagation

The easiest method is by division in spring.

Dionaea muscipula

SOME POPULAR SPECIES	
D. muscipula (USA) A rosette-forming carnivore with modified leaves with two halves bent upwards, the margins covered with long hairs,	and the centre of the 'pads' covered with reddish digestive glands. The plant may produce small heads of white flowers in summer.

Dracaena

PS/W/HH–MH

A most important group of houseplants, most being bold, 'architectural' in shape, and very striking. They are not beginners' plants, but with a little care they should have a reasonable life expectancy in the home.

How to grow

Never let the compost dry out, even in winter, and water freely in summer. Although *D. godseffiana* will tolerate dry air, the others listed below should be misted regularly. Keep away from a cold window at night in winter.

Dracaena godseffiana

Repot in spring when necessary using a soil-based compost. Feed fortnightly in summer. Any flowers which appear should be removed as soon as possible.

Propagation

Stem cuttings about 5–7.5 cm (2–3 in) long can be taken in spring or summer. To be more certain of success, use a rooting hormone and a propagator (even if the outside temperature is warm in summer, a propagator should provide the necessary humidity too).

Sections of bare stem with a couple of eyes can be cut up and rooted as eye cuttings.

If you just want to salvage a plant that has become leggy, try air layering it.

Cuttings of variegated dracaenas may produce green leaves at first, but coloured ones should develop later.

SOME POPULAR SPECIES

D. deremensis (Tropical Africa)
Forms a tuft of long, broad, arching dark green leaves with longitudinal silver stripes. There are varieties with variations in the variegation, 'Warneckii' being a popular one.
D. fragrans (Guinea and West Africa)
Like the above but the leaves are longer and broader. Again there are several varieties, mainly with creamy-yellow longitudinal stripes.

D. godseffiana (Congo)
Quite unlike the other dracaenas. Its leaves are more like those of the polka-dot plant (hypoestes—page 56) only with cream spots. It has a sprawling habit.
D. marginata *(Cordyline marginata)* (Madagascar)
Very colourful narrow leaves, striped red, cream, and green in the variety 'Tricolor'.
D. sanderiana (Congo)
A species with long, broad, leaves edged with a broad silvery-white band.

Echinocactus

FS/C/LH

Echinocactus grusonii

The Latin name comes from the Greek word *echinos,* meaning hedgehog—the spines are enough to justify the name, but the ball shape also resembles a rolled-up hedgehog.

How to grow

Good light is essential for good results. Water normally during the summer and feed occasionally. Keep practically dry and avoid too much warmth during the winter.

Use a loam-based or cactus compost when repotting. Be careful when repotting as the roots break easily.

Propagation

Can be raised from seed, but this is for the enthusiast and it is more sensible to try this if you have a greenhouse.

SOME POPULAR SPECIES

E. grusonii (Mexico) (Hedgehog cactus, golden barrel cactus). A spherical cactus, becoming more barrel-shaped with age. The dark green body has many ribs bristling with golden spines. The yellow flowers are unlikely to appear in the home.

E. ingens (Mexico) (Hedgehog cactus) Barrel-shaped, blue-grey body. Numerous spiny ribs and a woolly crown. There are several varieties although some of them may be available listed as distinct species.

Epiphyllum
Orchid cactus
PS/C/MH

In the wild there are about 21 species, with natural habitats in Central and South America, and especially Mexico, and the plants that we grow today are almost always hybrids of very mixed parentage. In the wild they grow as epiphytes. In the home they make ungainly houseplants out of flower, but the very large blooms are so spectacular that you may be inclined to put up with them for the 11 uninteresting months.

How to grow
Best out of doors for the summer, in a sheltered place out of direct sunlight. Bring indoors at the end of summer and keep the plant cool and the compost just moist enough to prevent it drying out.

Water freely and start feeding once the buds begin to form. Maintain a humid atmosphere once growth begins until they have finished flowering.

Repot only when really necessary. And avoid turning or moving once the buds have formed— they will probably drop.

Propagation
Cuttings root easily (roots may even appear from joints spontaneously if the atmosphere is humid enough, and in a greenhouse border the arching stems sometimes root themselves where they come into contact with the soil). Cut the stems into about 10 cm (4 in) sections and let them dry for a day or two before inserting into the compost.

SOME POPULAR SPECIES	
Epiphyllum hybrids The plants grown in the home are garden hybrids. The flowers may be 10–15 cm (4–6 in) across in	shades of red or yellow, or white. The long, notched stems are leaf-like, sometimes triangular in outline.

Erica
Heather/Cape heath
PS/C/MH

The garden heather is a well-known and popular garden plant, but the ericas grown as houseplants are tender species. They are not easy to grow on to flower another year because after the treatment they receive to induce them to flower for Christmas the plants are likely to deteriorate.

How to grow
You will probably buy the plant in bloom around

Erica hiemalis

Christmas time. Keep it in a cool, light position to prolong the flowering period.

To try to keep the plant for another year, use soft water, and if repotting use a lime-free compost. Stand the plant outside for the summer, being sure to keep it well watered. Feed fortnightly from late spring to mid summer and bring indoors before the first frost.

Propagation
The chances of growing a worthwhile plant from a cutting are not good (unless you have a greenhouse where they can be brought on for a year or two), but you can take cuttings in late summer. Use a rooting hormone.

SOME POPULAR SPECIES	
E. gracilis (South Africa) Typical small tubular heather flowers, usually rose-purple and produced during autumn and winter.	**E. hiemalis** (Origin uncertain) Similar to above. Flowers salmon-pink, rose-red, or white, usually pink flushed white.

Euonymus
PS–FS/C/MH–LH

The species used as indoor pot-plants are in fact hardy shrubs in most areas, and once the plants become too large indoors you can try planting them outdoors.

How to grow
Good light is essential for strong variegation, and to prevent legginess. They can stand outdoors, perhaps on the patio, for the summer.

Cut back long shoots in spring to maintain a bushy habit. Feed fortnightly during the summer.

Propagation
Take cuttings in spring or summer. They should root easily but it is worth using a rooting hormone. It is worth growing them outdoors or in a frame until they make respectably-sized pot-plants.

SOME POPULAR SPECIES	
E. japonicus (Japan) Glossy, leathery, oval leaves about 2.5–5 cm (1–2 in) long, dark green in the species. It is, however, the variegated forms that are used as houseplants. Upright,	shrubby habit. The varieties usually grown are 'Ovatus Aureus' (edged gold, paler in poor light), and 'Microphyllus', which has leaves about half the size and usually white variegation.

Euonymus japonicus 'Ovatus Aureus'

Euphorbia
Poinsettia
PS/W/HH

There are about 2,000 species of euphorbia. A few succulent types are sometimes used as houseplants, but there is just one that has to take pride of place—the very popular poinsettia *(E. pulcherrima)*. It is a traditional Christmas gift plant but will seldom give a satisfactory display another year. The treatment that poinsettias receive from commercial growers—artificial light early in the season to interrupt the night, then gradually decreasing day lengths within an artificial black-out, special temperature control, and dwarfing by use of growth inhibitors—means that you have no hope of achieving a repeat performance next year.

How to grow
If bought in flower (actually the red 'petals' are bracts, the proper flowers are the insignificant parts in the middle), maintain a steady temperature, and mist the plants regularly.

If you want to keep the plant, cut the shoots back to half their length after flowering (dust cut surfaces with charcoal), and repot. Feed from the end of summer until the flower buds start to show.

Flowers will not form until the day length is reduced to about 10 hours (you can adjust this artificially or wait for nature, but do not keep the plant in a room where you are going to turn on the light!). When it does flower, the plant will be taller, less compact, than when you bought it.

Propagation
Stem cuttings can be taken in spring or summer. Dip the cut ends into charcoal or a rooting powder to stop the flow of sap. Cuttings taken in spring will probably need the aid of a propagator.

SOME POPULAR SPECIES	
E. pulcherrima (Mexico) Needs no description.	The bracts are usually red but may be pink or white.

Exacum
Persian violet
PS/(W)/MH

Only an annual, so it must be discarded after flowering, but a charming plant especially useful because it is available through the autumn and into winter. Although the flowers are usually described as fragrant, do not expect too much—you will have to sniff at close quarters. If you are buying a plant, choose one which has plenty of buds still to open so you will have it for the maximum time possible.

Exacum affine

How to grow
If you buy a plant in flower there are few problems: just keep it out of direct sunshine (which may scorch the leaves) and make sure the compost never dries out. Turn the pot a quarter turn each day to ensure an even display, and remove dead flowers regularly.

Propagation
Easily raised from seed if you have a greenhouse, but the plants are likely to become drawn if they have spent their whole life indoors. Best sown in spring, and they will make a better display if you put several plants to a pot and pinch out the growing tips a few times to encourage branching and a bushy habit.

SOME POPULAR SPECIES	
E. affine (Socotra) Small oval, glossy green leaves on a bushy plant covered with small lilac-	blue flowers set off by a central boss of yellow stamens. They are slightly fragrant.

x *Fatshedera*
PS/C/MH

An interesting as well as useful plant. It is a bigeneric cross between *Fatsia japonica* (see next) and *Hedera helix* 'Hibernica', an ivy—(see page 52). Crosses between genera are unusual and this one was made in 1912 on the French nursery of Lizé Frères at Nantes. It combines some of the best features of both parents.

How to grow
Water regularly from spring to autumn, sparingly in winter. Mist the leaves regularly and frequently.

The stems can be trained upwards around a cane or allowed to hang down. If you want to encourage the plant to branch, then pinch out the growing tip.

Repot each spring and feed monthly in summer.

Propagation
Stem cuttings taken in summer.

SOME POPULAR SPECIES	
x F. lizei (Garden origin) A leafy semi-climber with large three- or five-lobed leaves. The stems grow upwards initially then flop	and become recumbent. The normal form is green, but 'Variegata', which grows more slowly, has white-edged leaves.

x *Fatshedera lizei*

Fatsia
False castor oil plant
PS/C/MH

Fatsia japonica

This tough foliage plant has been grown as a houseplant for more than 150 years, yet it still deserves to be better known. It will make a fine specimen plant of perhaps 1.2 m (4 ft) or more for a living-room or even a cool hallway.

The plant is hardy outdoors in mild areas.

How to grow
Best in a light position in winter, but avoid direct sun. Water freely in summer, sparingly in winter. Makes a useful patio plant for the summer, but keep it out of strong sunlight. Avoid too much heat in winter.

Mist frequently, and sponge the leaves with water occasionally. Repot each spring.

Propagation
Stem cuttings can be taken in summer. If you have a greenhouse it might be worth sowing seeds in spring.

SOME POPULAR SPECIES
F. japonica (Japan) Large, hand-like leaves with seven to nine lobes held out on long stalks. Mature plants may have white flower heads in late autumn or early winter, but this is unlikely indoors. The ordinary species is green, but 'Variegata' is splashed white. This is the only species.

Ficus
(large-leaved species)
PS/W/MH

There are more than 800 species of *Ficus*, and as one would expect in a group of that size some of them are very diverse in appearance. Some are delicate, small-leaved creeping plants (some small-leaved species are listed on page 47), others are large-leaved and will make trees in their native habitat. Of the large-leaved species the rubber plant (*Ficus elastica*) is the most widely known and grown, though now in improved forms, but there are many other species that are worth growing for a dramatic and ornamental effect.

Ficus benjamina

How to grow
Be careful not to overwater; make sure the compost is becoming dry first. Mist occasionally in summer. Sponge the leaves occasionally with water. Feed fortnightly from spring to autumn.

Propagation
If you simply want to replace a plant that has become leggy, air layering is likely to be the answer.

Tips and sideshoots can be used as cuttings. Dip the cut end and dust the cut on the plant with charcoal to stop the flow of latex.

Stems can be used to provide eye cuttings. Make these by cutting the stem into sections about 2.5 cm (1 in) long with a leaf and an eye (bud). If the leaf is large, as with *F. elastica* for instance, it is usual to roll the leaf up and pop an elastic band round it, to reduce water loss from the leaf.

SOME POPULAR SPECIES
F. benjamina (India) (Weeping fig) Leathery, glossy green leaves which tend to hang down. There is a variegated form 'Hawaii'.
F. deltoidea *(F. diversifolia)* (India, Malaysia) (Mistletoe fig) A slow-growing, branching plant. The leathery leaves have a blunt tip and tapering base. Pea-sized pseudo-fruits appear throughout the year, even on young plants.
F. elastica (Tropical Asia) (Rubber plant) As a houseplant it is usually seen as a single unbranched stem with large glossy green leaves. The true species is now seldom seen as its varieties are better. These include 'Decora' (deeper green, red coloration on underside); 'Robusta' (broader leaves than 'Decora' and more compact); 'Schrijveriana' (yellow-green and dark green patterning). There are several more.
F. lyrata (West Africa) (Fiddle-back fig) Large, glossy dark green violin-shaped leaves with slightly paler sunken veins.

Ficus
(small-leaved species)
PS–SH/W/MH–HH

Ficus radicans 'Variegata'

The large-leaved ficus are mentioned in the previous entry, the species described here are the creeping figs, which are very different in scale and habit, and also need more care to grow. They are frequently used in hanging pots, but *F. pumila* will also scramble upwards if it has something to cling to.

How to grow
These plants enjoy good light but direct sunlight will soon cause problems. Water freely in the warm months, cautiously otherwise. Mist regularly. Feed periodically in summer.

Propagation
These species are best raised from stem cuttings, but they really need the warmth and humidity of a propagator if possible. Use a rooting hormone.

SOME POPULAR SPECIES
F. pumila *(F. repens)* (China) (Creeping fig) The immature leaves (mature leaves are seldom seen) are small and heart-shaped, with prominent veins. Will climb, using clinging roots. 'Variegata', marbled white, tends to revert to green.
F. radicans (East Indies) (Trailing fig) A trailing plant best in a hanging pot. Lance-shaped, pointed leaves, edged and blotched creamy-white in the variety 'Variegata'.

Fittonia

PS/H/HH

Beautiful creeping foliage plant from the rain forests of Peru, but sadly among the more difficult houseplants.

How to grow

The key to success is moist but not waterlogged compost in summer (water sparingly in winter), and a humid environment—mist daily. Feed weekly from spring to autumn. The small-leaved *F. verschaffeltii* 'Argyroneura Nana' seems to be more tolerant than the large-leaved forms.

They do not make a large root system and usually look better in a half-pot or other shallow container in a peat-based compost.

Propagation

Cuttings taken in spring or summer should root, but as the plant tends to creep and root on its own you may find it easier to divide a large plant.

SOME POPULAR SPECIES
F. verschaffeltii (Peru) (Painted net leaf, mosaic plant) Creeping stems with oval leaves about 7.5–10 cm (3–4 in) long, carmine veins being the attractive feature. The variety 'Argyroneura' (often listed as a distinct species; common name silver net leaf) has silvery veins. 'Argyroneura Nana', the snakeskin plant, also has silvery veins, but the leaves are only about 2.5 cm (1 in) long. It is an easier form to grow.

Fittonia 'Argyroneura Nana'

Gloxinia

PS/(W)/HH

This should strictly be included under *Sinningia*, for its correct name is *S. speciosa*, but plants are sold almost everywhere under their old name of gloxinia which is why they have been included here. The modern varieties are very beautiful, but the home is a far from ideal place for them.

How to grow

Avoid bright sunlight but a light position is essential. Never let the compost dry out during the growing season, provide as much humidity as possible, but avoid wetting the leaves. Feed every week during the summer.

Gloxinia (*Sinningia speciosa*)

The plant will die down in the autumn. Let the compost dry out completely once the leaves turn yellow. Store the tuber in a frost-free place. In spring repot the tuber (make sure the hollow side is uppermost), keep the compost just moist, and put in a warm place until the tuber starts to grow. Then treat as before.

Propagation
If you have a greenhouse they can be raised from seed, but indoors this is not likely to be worth the effort. Take leaf cuttings in early summer.

SOME POPULAR SPECIES	
G. speciosa *(Sinningia speciosa)* (Brazil) Almost stemless hairy leaves up to 25 cm (10 in) long. The large bell-	shaped flowers are stalked and upward-pointing. There are many varieties in colours that include red, pink, purple, white.

Grevillea
Silk bark oak
PS/C/MH

This evergreen shrub is sometimes used as a 'spot' or accent plant in formal summer bedding schemes, but it makes an attractive houseplant too. For a cool bright spot it will make a useful large specimen, though the plants are frequently discarded by the time they reach 90 cm (3 ft) because the foliage tends to deteriorate. When allowed to grow to its full size in its native Australia and other warm climate countries, grevillea produces a mass of deep golden flowers—unfortunately never seen on the houseplant.

How to grow
Although the plant should not be in direct mid-day sunlight in summer, it will benefit from good light in winter. There is no need to feed, but repot young plants in spring.

Water well from late spring to autumn but keep the plant a little drier in the winter.

Propagation
Easily raised from seed sown in spring or summer. Cuttings can be taken from sideshoots in spring or late summer.

SOME POPULAR SPECIES	
G. robusta (New South Wales) Feathery, fern-like	bipinnate or tripinnate foliage, the young leaves covered with silky hairs.

Grevillea robusta

Guzmania
PS/W/HH

A group of bromeliads, named after A. Guzman an 18th century Spanish botanist and apothecary, native mainly to the tropical rain forests of South America.

How to grow
Use tepid, soft water for watering and misting. From spring until early autumn keep the central vase topped up with water. During the growing season, a very dilute fertiliser can be poured into the vase. After flowering, when the plants begin to rest, leave the vase empty.

Mist frequently while the flowers are developing.

Propagation
Detach offsets from around the parent plant. But wait until they are quite large and detach with a portion of root. Keep warm until the offsets have become established.

SOME POPULAR SPECIES	
G. lingulata (Colombia) Narrow, bright green, glossy leaves growing rosette-fashion to form a vase. Bright red bracts, with a cluster of yellowish flowers in the centre. There are many hybrids	derived from this species. **G. minor** (Costa Rica, Panama, Brazil) Similar to above, but a smaller plant (about 25 cm/10 in tall) with white flowers in the red or orange bracts.

Top *Guzmania lingulata*
Bottom *Guzmania minor*

Haworthia fasciata

Gynura
Purple passion vine
PS/W/MH

Gynura procumbens

The gynuras grown as houseplants are attractive because of their unusual colouring. The leaves are covered with purple hairs, the effect of which varies according to the light and angle of view.

How to grow
Good light is needed to retain good colouring and to prevent the plant becoming leggy, but avoid direct midday sunlight. Pinch back regularly to maintain a branching, bushy plant. Water freely in summer, sparingly in winter.

Old plants become straggly indoors so it is best to take cuttings to maintain a supply of young plants.

Propagation
Cuttings root easily, especially in spring.

SOME POPULAR SPECIES	
G. procumbens *(G. sarmentosa)* (India) A trailing plant, the dark green leaves thickly covered with purple hairs.	Pale orange, insignificant flowers may appear, but you may find the smell unpleasant and prefer to remove them.

Haworthia
Wart plant
PS/C/LH

Small succulents grown for their thickened, attractively marked leaves, arranged as a rosette. Most species are covered with white warts.

How to grow
Although these plants need good light, they are best out of direct sun, which colours their leaves and makes them less attractive. Water normally in summer, sparingly in winter. Feeding is not normally necessary.

Propagation
The simplest way is to remove the offsets that usually form freely.

SOME POPULAR SPECIES	
H. attenuata (South Africa) Narrow, fleshy leaves with bands of white warts on the back. Forms rosettes. **H. fasciata** (South Africa) Fleshy, pointed, incurving leaves with white warts on	the lower surface (the side usually seen). **H. margaritifera** (South Africa) Similar to *H. fasciata*, but the rosettes are broader and the warts distributed more randomly.

Hedera

Ivy
PS–SH/C/MH

The ivies need no introduction—the common *H. helix* is found wild in Britain and other parts of Europe. They are tough plants, but still need a modicum of care to make good houseplants.

How to grow

Avoid hot, stuffy rooms. Use ivies for the cooler parts of the home, although *H. canariensis* will tolerate more warmth than *H. helix*. Green varieties will tolerate poor light, but variegated kinds need good light. Never allow the compost to dry out. Mist regularly if warm and dry.

Propagation

Very easy to propagate—cuttings will even root in water (though it is advisable to insert them in compost). You can also layer stems into small pots of compost near the parent plant.

When they have rooted, put several young plants in one pot and pinch out the growing tips.

SOME POPULAR SPECIES	
H. canariensis (Canary Islands) (Canary Island ivy) The species has green leaves, but 'Variegata' (also known as 'Gloire de Marengo') is the one used as a houseplant. This has large, heart-shaped leaves margined or blotched white or silver-grey. **H. helix** (Europe)	(Ivy) The species needs no description, but it is the various small-leaved varieties that are grown as houseplants. These are either variegated (usually with cream or yellow) or have a distinctive leaf shape. There are many of these varieties, but treatment is similar for all of them.

Hedera canariensis 'Variegata'

Helxine

Mind your own business/ baby's tears
PS/C/MH

A genus with only one species, a diminutive plant but useful for cool spots around the home. Its correct name is now *Soleirolia soleirolii*, but as it is still more often sold under the name *H. soleirolii* it

Helxine soleirolii, H.s. 'Argentea', *H.s.* 'Aurea'

has been included under that name here.

How to grow

The plant will actually stand some frost, and thrives better in a cool room than one that is hot and stuffy. The plant will shrivel and collapse if you once let the compost dry out, so water whenever necessary. Misting will help to provide the humid environment that it prefers.

The plant roots as it spreads over the surface of the compost, so it will need annual repotting, preferably using a wide but shallow container.

Propagation

Simply divide the clump or just tease off some rooted stems from around the edge, preferably in spring or summer.

SOME POPULAR SPECIES	
H. soleirolii *(Soleirolia soleirolii)* (Corsica) This dense little creeper has round, pale green leaves about 6 mm (¼ in)	across. The variety 'Argentea' has silvery foliage. 'Aurea' has attractive yellowish-green leaves.

Hibiscus

Rose mallow/rose of China
PS–FS/W/MH

There are hardy hibiscus, but the species grown as a houseplant is *H. rosa-sinensis*, a Chinese shrub with huge, colourful blooms, persuaded by commercial growers to appear even on small, compact plants. Growth-retardant chemicals are used, so do not expect the same results from your own cuttings.

How to grow

This is a plant that needs a position in good light. Keep the compost moist at all times, but reduce the amount of water given in winter. Mist the plant occasionally, and feed from mid summer to late autumn.

Prune back long stems in late winter, to induce bushiness, and repot in late spring.

Propagation

Tip cuttings are usually taken between mid spring and early autumn. A propagator will help.

SOME POPULAR SPECIES	
H. rosa-sinensis (China) Glossy green, oval leaves, toothed near the pointed tip. Large single, semi-double or double flowers about 7.5–10 cm (3–4 in)	across, in shades of crimson, pink, yellow, or white, with prominent stamens. Several varieties are available, most of them hybrids.

Hibiscus rosa-sinensis

Hippeastrum
Amaryllis
FS/W/MH

There is another plant known as amaryllis—*A. belladonna,* a bulb sometimes grown outdoors and never used as a houseplant—but the name has become attached to the hippeastrum that is such a popular gift plant (as a dry bulb) at Christmas. Hippeastrums are stunning and easy-to-grow plants.

Hippeastrum

How to grow
Plant a dry bulb in a 15 cm (6 in) pot, leaving half the bulb exposed. Moisten the compost, and place the pot in a warm place—near a radiator if necessary. Take care not to overwater nor to saturate the compost, then a shoot should soon appear. When it is about 15 cm (6 in) tall, move the pot to a light place, and water freely. Feed fortnightly.

After flowering, remove the flowering stem, gradually reduce the amount of water and let the foliage die down. Start into growth again when a new shoot appears in early spring.

Propagation
You can propagate hippeastrums at home, but it takes a long time. A large parent bulb will produce offset bulbs that will develop their own roots. These can be removed and grown on in their own pots. They might flower after about three years.

SOME POPULAR SPECIES	
Hippeastrum hybrids (Garden origin) The hippeastrums grown as houseplants are hybrids. Strap-shaped green leaves are topped by	stout flowering stems sometimes 60 cm (2 ft) high with clusters of large funnel-shaped flowers. Colours include reds, pinks, and white.

Hyacinthus
Hyacinth
PS/C/MH

The hyacinth was named after *Hyakinthos,* a beautiful boy loved by Apollo and accidentally killed by him. The bold flowers and fragrance make the hyacinth a much-loved flower.

How to grow
Hyacinths are not houseplants but are forced to provide winter decoration indoors. Afterwards they should be planted in the garden.

For Christmas flowering you must buy 'prepared' bulbs and plant as soon as possible.

Hyacinthus orientalis

You can use bulb fibre in containers without drainage, ordinary compost in pots with a drainage hole. Leave 1 cm (½ in) of the bulb above the surface.

Place in a cool dark place (ideally outside covered with a layer of peat). Check occasionally to ensure the compost has not dried out. When the shoots are 2.5–5 cm (1–2 in) high, bring them into a cool room (about 10°C/50°F). Leave them in a shady position for the first few days, then put in a light place.

Propagation

Hyacinths for forcing need specialist techniques, not a practical proposition for an amateur.

SOME POPULAR SPECIES	
H. orientalis (Eastern Europe, Western Asia) The species is no longer grown. It is the large-flowered hybrids that are	used. These are too well known to need description. There are many varieties in a range of colours.

Hydrangea
PS/C/MH–HH

The hydrangeas are useful garden shrubs, and it is easy to overlook their potential as houseplants. Commercially they are forced into flower early by inducing dormancy by defoliating the plants (the method varies from placing ripe apples in a sealed store with the plants—the apples release ethylene gas—to chemical defoliants sprayed onto the plants). There are various other processes through which they have to pass, sometimes including the use of growth inhibitors to keep the plants compact, before they are offered for sale. So your own efforts are unlikely to be as successful.

How to grow

Keep the compost moist at all times during the growing season, using soft water. Mist the leaves occasionally.

If you do raise your own plants you may have to use a proprietary blueing compound (follow the manufacturer's instructions) to avoid some varieties coming out pink. Colour depends partly on variety and partly on soil or compost (or in some cases what you add to it).

Feed the plants weekly when they start to grow in spring and again in summer after the plants have rested.

Avoid a hot, dry atmosphere at any time, but especially when the plants are in flower. After flowering, cut the stems back by half.

Propagation

It is not advisable to try raising new hydrangeas

Hydrangea macrophylla

indoors. But if you want to try, take 'half ripe' cuttings (not soft and not woody) in summer—they will even root in water. The young plants will need stopping a couple of times, and you must expect to wait until the third year for flowers.

SOME POPULAR SPECIES	
H. macrophylla *(H. hortensis)* (China, Japan) Broad oval, toothed leaves, up to 15 cm (6 in) long. Large globular flower heads, blue, pink or white depending on the variety and the acidity of the	compost. Some varieties are described as 'Lacecaps', the inner florets being fertile, only those round the edge being sterile and therefore having the decorative petals.

Hypocyrta
Clog plant
FS–PS/W/MH

Most species have their natural home in the Brazilian jungles. Only one of them is used as a houseplant, and even this can be a straggly, not very attractive plant for most of the year. The flowers are small and tend to be hidden among the foliage, but the plant can look attractive in flower if well grown.

How to grow
Will take some direct sun, especially in winter. Water freely in summer and mist periodically. Feed fortnightly in summer.

Cut the stems back in winter to improve the shape and to encourage more flowering growth.

Propagation
Take cuttings in spring or summer.

SOME POPULAR SPECIES
H. glabra (South America) Small, dark green, leathery, glossy, green leaves. Orange waxy flowers with a tube oddly bulged at the base.

Hypocyrta glabra

Hypoestes
Polka-dot plant
PS/W/HH

There is some confusion over the name of the species sold as a houseplant—*H. phyllostachya* is the correct name, but it is almost always sold under its old name of *H. sanguinolenta*. However, some authorities give this name to a plant without blotched leaves (very unlikely to be encountered). It matters little for the plants sold are very appealing and a tempting buy. Be warned however, that they have probably been treated with a dwarfing chemical which will wear off and the plants will soon become leggy and unattractive in the poor light conditions indoors.

Hypoestes phyllostachya

How to grow
Good light coupled with high humidity will produce the best plants. Mist the leaves frequently and repot in spring—if you decide to keep an old plant (it is best to raise new plants from cuttings). Pinch back leggy growth to encourage bushiness.

Propagation
Cuttings root easily in spring or summer if you provide a humid environment. You can buy seed, but this is best used if you have a greenhouse.

Even then the colouring and marking may not be as good as some vegetatively-propagated strains.

SOME POPULAR SPECIES	
H. phyllostachya *(H. sanguinolenta)* (Madagascar) Oval, pointed leaves about 7 cm (2½ in) long, green spotted and blotched pink. The intensity of colour	and the amount of marking (some are predominantly pink with little green showing) depend on a combination of light, nutrient levels, and the variety.

Impatiens
Busy Lizzie
PS–FS/W/MH

In the days before there was a wide choice of houseplants, the busy Lizzie was very popular indoors. It has fallen out of favour to some extent, which is a pity because the modern varieties are vast improvements on the old ones, and generally much more compact.

How to grow
Intense midday summer sun should be avoided, otherwise good light is needed to keep the plants compact.

Keep the compost moist at all times in the summer, but water cautiously in winter. Mist occasionally. Feed weekly in summer.

The plants eventually become leggy or untidy, so propagate a supply of fresh plants each year.

Propagation
Most impatiens are raised from seed, but ideally you need a warm, light place if the seedlings are to do well. Sow in spring to give the young plants chance to become established in the good light of summer.

Cuttings root very easily, even in water. Spring or summer is a good time to take them. Some varieties with variegated foliage can only be raised from cuttings.

Remove the growing tips from young plants to encourage bushiness.

SOME POPULAR SPECIES	
I. walleriana *(I. holstii)* (East Africa) Branching, slightly translucent, fleshy stems, bright green elliptical leaves. Flowers flat, five-petalled, about 2.5 cm (1 in) across. The species itself is not grown	and the varieties used are mainly hybrids between this species and *I. sultanii*. Choose compact varieties for indoors. There are double as well as single varieties, and most New Guinea hybrids have variegated leaves.

Impatiens New Guinea hybrid

Iris

PS–FS/C/LH

Iris reticulata 'Harmony'

Irises are not really houseplants, but some of the dwarf species are useful for a late winter display indoors.

How to grow
Plant the bulbs in pots of ordinary compost in early autumn, then leave outdoors, covered with peat or grit, until the shoots are about 2.5 cm (1 in) high. Bring into the light, ideally into a greenhouse or garden frame if you want early flowers, but only into the house once colour is showing.

The bulbs should be planted in the garden afterwards to flower in future years.

It is best to buy new bulbs for an indoor display.

Propagation
The bulbs will multiply themselves, but they might take a couple of years to flower and they are best planted out in the garden. For a dependable indoor display it is worth buying flowering-sized bulbs each year.

SOME POPULAR SPECIES	
I. danfordiae (Eastern Turkey) Yellow fragrant flowers appear almost before the leaves. Height about 10 cm (4 in) although the leaves will exceed this later. Flowers mid or late winter.	**I. reticulata** (Russia, Caucasus, Northern Persia). Blue or purple flowers (depending on variety), similar to above species, but not fragrant. Height about 13 cm (5 in). Mid to late winter.

Jasminum

FS/C/MH–HH

The jasmines used as houseplants are not entirely happy indoors, but as sold they make attractive plants, looped round a cane or wire.

How to grow
Good light is important, and frequent mistings will help to keep the jasmine in good condition. Never let the compost dry out.

Jasminum polyanthum

In summer, jasmines can stand outside, but make sure they are kept watered. Bring them indoors before the first frost.

After flowering, prune to keep the plants reasonably compact (they are climbers) and to encourage flowering. Repot in spring when necessary.

Propagation
Stem cuttings should root if taken in spring or autumn, but use a rooting hormone.

Kalanchoe
(flowering type)
PS–FS/W/MH–LH

Kalanchoe blossfeldiana

The best-known kalanchoes are the flowering *K. blossfeldiana* hybrids, some of the less decorative but nevertheless fascinating viviparous species are described on page 60.

By using blackouts and supplementary lighting as necessary, commercial growers can induce them to flower at any time of year (they flower only after a period of short days). The day length required varies to some extent according to variety, and out of season flowering is not a job for the amateur. The plants you buy may also have been treated with a growth regulator to improve the shape and appearance of the plant and to ensure compactness—you will not be able to achieve the same results at home. You can keep the plants compact by pinching out the growing tips of small plants, but this will delay flowering by about three weeks and isn't successful with all varieties.

How to grow
Water moderately in summer, a little more sparingly in winter. Feeding once a month should be adequate.

Bought plants should remain in flower for a month or two. They will flower again another year, but probably bloom at a different time and be more straggly.

If you want to keep the plant, cut back the stem to one pair of leaves after flowering, and repot. Once the plant starts growing again, feed until the flowers appear, usually in spring.

Propagation
Take cuttings in spring or summer. Let them dry for a day before inserting into the compost. Can also be raised from seed.

SOME POPULAR SPECIES

K. blossfeldiana (Madagascar) (Flaming Katy) Leathery, glossy green leaves, brittle and easily broken. Clusters of short-stalked flowers, usually scarlet in the species, but in the hybrids the flower colours range from red, through orange to yellow, and even lilac.

K. manginii (Madagascar) Lance-shaped to spatula-shaped leaves 2–4 cm (¾–1½ in) long. The pendulous red flowers grow in small clusters suspended above the foliage.
A much less popular species than *K. blossfeldiana.*

Kalanchoe
(viviparous type)
PS–FS/W/LH

Popular flowering species are described on page 59. Those described below are the fascinating viviparous species that produce miniature plants along or at the end of the leaves—instant plants that make propagation exceedingly easy (they will fall off anyway and root in the pot).

These species were previously listed under the genus *Bryophyllum*, and this name is still used by some growers.

How to grow
These succulent plants will not come to much harm even if the compost dries out occasionally, but they will grow more lushly if watered normally during the summer. To keep the plants small, resist the temptation to feed.

These plants can eventually become tall and leggy, and although the flowers they then produce are not unattractive, the plant as a whole will begin to look ungainly by that stage. It is much better to discard old plants and grow on some of the inevitable supply of young plants.

Kalanchoe diagremontiana

Propagation
Simply pot up the small plantlets.

SOME POPULAR SPECIES	
K. daigremontiana *(Bryophyllum daigremontianum)* (Madagascar) Long, triangular leaves, green but with purple markings on the back; the base clasping the stem. Plantlets form along the edge of each mature leaf.	There is little branching, and the plant usually grows on a single stem. **K. tubiflora** *(Bryophyllum tubiflorum)* (Madagascar) Lacks recognisable leaves, as they are cylindrical and resemble stems, green with darker markings. Plantlets form at the tips.

Kentia
PS/W/MH

In many books you will find the Kentia Palms listed under the new and more correct name of *Howeia* (sometimes written *Howea*), but others still use *Kentia*, a name under which they are still likely to be sold.

How to grow
Keep just moist at all times, letting the plants almost dry out between waterings in winter. Try to mist daily in summer, when the plants should be fed fortnightly. Sponge the leaves with clean water occasionally.

Kentia forsteriana

Repot when necessary, probably every other spring, using a peat- or soil-based compost.

Propagation
By seed, but not really a practical proposition in the home. Suckers may be produced and these can be removed when repotting and grown on individually.

SOME POPULAR SPECIES	
K. belmoreana *(Howeia belmoreana)* (Lord Howe Islands) Dark green, arching pinnate leaves with long linear leaflets. **K. forsteriana** *(Howeia forsteriana)* (Lord Howe Islands)	Similar to above, but with more drooping fronds with fewer leaflets. The fronds unfurl slowly, and growth is slow, producing perhaps only one new leaf in a year. For this reason several plants are usually grown in the same pot.

Lilium
Lily
PS–FS/C/MH

Although lilies have long been popular pot plants in the USA, in Britain and many other European countries it has only been with the increasing use of growth regulators that they have become a more important commercial crop. These help to reduce the stem to a more acceptable height. Lilies are very difficult pot plants to attempt to raise yourself indoors (it is even difficult for commercial growers) and they are best bought in flower, used as a room decoration, and then planted in the garden.

How to grow
Keep in good light and water freely. Once the flowers fade, remove the dead head and plant out in the garden.

Growing your own from bought bulbs, or growing on the old bulb, needs better light than you can expect in the home.

Propagation
Not suitable for the amateur for growing as a houseplant.

SOME POPULAR SPECIES	
In Europe Mid-Century hybrids are usually used, particularly the varieties 'Enchantment' and	'Destiny'. In the USA the *L. longiflorum* varieties 'Ace' and 'Nellie White' are also popular.

Lilium 'Enchantment'

Lithops
Living stone/pebble plant
FS/C/LH

A genus of about 50 species of intriguing succulents consist of a pair of thickened leaves united at the base. They present a flattened top that resembles the stones of their native desert—a form of mimicry that protects them from their natural enemies. From the narrow slit between the leaves, two new leaves are produced, absorbing the sap from the old pair. Colourful, daisy-like flowers may appear from the slit. Use a loam-based or cactus compost when repotting.

How to grow
These plants need the best possible light and plenty of sun. Very little water is needed—none at all from mid autumn until spring when the new leaves break out. In summer they are best watered from the base to reduce the risk of rotting.

Propagation
Seed germinates easily, but the plants take two or three years to flower. Sow in spring.

Lithops

SOME POPULAR SPECIES	
L. lesliei (Namaqualand) Rusty-brown upper surface with a network of greenish-brown grooves. Yellow flowers. **L. pseudotruncatella** (Namaqualand) Light brown, mottled dark	brown, leaves. Yellow flowers, and one of the easiest to induce to flower. **L. turbiniformis** (Namaqualand) Brownish-grey leaves with dark brown markings.

Lithops

Lobivia

Lobivia
FS/C/LH

There are not many plant names that are anagrams, but *Lobivia* is an anagram of Bolivia, which is where most of these cacti originate. They are grown for their highly coloured flowers, which although short-lived are produced over a long period during the summer.

Use a loam-based or cactus compost when repotting.

How to grow
Lobivias need good light at all times and a cool position in winter. Water moderately in summer

but the compost should be kept practically dry from mid autumn until spring. Feed once a month in summer.

Propagation
Offsets can be detached when repotting; sometimes these already have roots on. Can also be increased by seed sown in a cactus seed mix.

SOME POPULAR SPECIES	
L. densispina (Peru) A densely thorned, short, cylindrical cactus. Red, orange or yellow funnel-shaped flowers about 5 cm	(2 in) across. **L. backebergii** (Bolivia) Round to oval stems with 15 notched ribs. Carmine flowers.

Mammillaria
FS/C/LH
A large group of spherical or columnar cacti, grown for their interesting shape or spines, and sometimes flowers (although these are small in some species).

How to grow
Good light and cautious watering are both important. Water only very sparingly in winter—withhold water completely if the temperature can be kept low. Repot each spring, using a loam-based or cactus compost.

Propagation
Offsets provide the easiest means of propagation.

SOME POPULAR SPECIES	
M. bocasana (Mexico) A clump-forming plant if left undisturbed, with fine white spines and silky hairs. Hooked thorns. Cream flowers. **M. bombycina** (Mexico) Cylindrical stems. Young areoles very woolly. Pale purple flowers. **M. elongata** (Mexico) Usually erect, cylindrical and very spiny stems forming a tight cluster. Small white, rather insignificant flowers. **M. hahniana** (Mexico) (Old lady cactus) Globular, clump-forming plant covered with long	hairs and white thorns. Funnel-shaped rose-red flowers arranged in a ring round the top. **M. prolifera** (West Indies) A round or cylindrical cactus that grows into a large cluster. Yellow flowers. A tough cactus that flowers easily. A good beginner's cactus. **M. zeilmanniana** (Mexico) (Rose pincushion) A cluster-forming plant, densely covered with white thorns. Bell-shaped deep violet-red or white flowers.

Top *Mammillaria bombycina*
Bottom *M. zeilmanniana*

Maranta
Prayer plant
PS/W/HH

Maranta leuconeura 'Kerchoveana'

Beautiful foliage plants, tempting to buy but unfortunately difficult to care for. Most of the marantas used as houseplants are varieties of *M. leuconeura*, a species from Brazil.

How to grow
Water freely from early spring to early autumn, moderately for the rest of the year. Feed fortnightly in summer. Use soft water, and mist the foliage frequently.

A peat-based compost seems to suit marantas, repot when necessary—probably every two years or so.

Remove leaves as soon as they fade. Smaller species do well in a bottle garden.

Propagation
Division in spring.

SOME POPULAR SPECIES	
M. leuconeura (Brazil) Oval leaves that stand upright and fold at night. Young leaves are green with purple-brown blotches between the lateral veins. Older leaves turn a greyer colour and the blotches darker. There are several varieties, three popular ones being 'Kerchoveana' (bright	green upper surface blotched dark green or dark purple), 'Massangeana' (dark green with white veins, the leaves pale purple beneath), and 'Erythrophylla' (yellow-green margins, dark green centres, and dark crimson mid-rib and veins).

Mimosa
Sensitive plant/humble plant
PS/H/MH

The plant described below is not the yellow-flowered tree known as mimosa *(Acacia dealbata)*, but a fascinating foliage plant grown mainly for amusement. The leaves are sensitive to touch and movement (the effect being most pronounced above about 24°C/75°F).

How to grow
Best grown as an annual. Keep moist at all times and feed fortnightly during the summer. The plants need good light but shade from intense summer sun.

Mist the leaves to maintain humidity and repot when necessary.

Mimosa pudica

Propagation

Cuttings can be taken, but as the plants become rather lank and unattractive in the home, they are usually raised from seed each year. Sow in spring. If you provide warmth, ideally in a propagator, the seeds should germinate reasonably readily.

M. pudica (Brazil) Pale green bipinnate leaves. Both the leaflets and leaf stalks fold and	droop if touched, resuming their normal position if left undisturbed for a while.

Monstera

Swiss cheese plant
PS–SH/W/HH–MH

Monstera deliciosa

Monsteras mainly belong to tropical America, and usually grow as epiphytes. The name was probably derived from the Latin *monstrum* meaning monstrosity. Perhaps once, with their slashed and holed leaves, they were considered monstrosities. Now they are regarded as highly desirable houseplants. They have an 'architectural' quality that makes them much valued as specimen plants standing alone.

The naming of the plants sold as monsteras is confused. *M. deliciosa* is sometimes offered as *Philodendron pertusum*, which is doubly confusing because there is a variety of *M. deliciosa* sometimes offered as *M. pertusa* (though it is more commonly known as *M. deliciosa* 'Borsigiana'). Do not let this confusion worry you: they are all desirable and similar houseplants.

How to grow

Monsteras will tolerate poor light, but they do much better in good light: the leaves will be bigger and healthier, with more holes. Aerial roots are produced, which will help to support the plant if you feed them into a moss pole. It may be possible to train some of them into the compost, but the plant will still grow even if you cut them off.

Feed fortnightly from spring to autumn, and repot each spring while the plant is still small.

The plants will exist with moderate humidity, but they will grow much better with regular misting and a humid atmosphere.

Propagation

If you just want to replace a leggy plant, air layering is the best solution. If you want more plants, cuttings from the tips of new shoots can be taken in summer. To produce a larger number of plants, stems can be made into eye cuttings (include a leaf, which can be rolled in the same way that rubber plant, *Ficus elastica*, leaves are rolled to reduce water loss).

M. deliciosa *(Philodendron pertusum)* (Mexico) Large green, glossy leaves, initially heart-shaped but becoming perforated. Mature leaves are about 60 cm (2 ft) across. The variety 'Borsigiana' is smaller, with leaves only	about half the size of the species. It is a more suitable plant for the home. **M. pertusa** *(M. adansonii)* (Tropical America) Similar to above, but leaves only about 30 cm (1 ft) across, and quite slow-growing.

Narcissus
Daffodil
PS/C/MH

Narcissus

Narcissi need no introduction, but flowering them in pots indoors is not as easy as one would think. Too much heat at the wrong time, or too little light, and the leaves and stems will become too tall and then flop and look untidy.

If you buy the plants in flower—or rather in bud, which is preferable—you should have no problems as they can be treated like long-lasting cut flowers, with the benefit of being able to plant the bulbs outdoors afterwards to flower in future years.

How to grow
Bulbs bought in pots as they are coming into flower pose no problem. Simply keep the compost moist; they will also last longer if kept in a cool position.

You can plant 'prepared' bulbs (for early flowering) in mid autumn, ordinary bulbs (to flower later) in early or mid autumn. Use pots of ordinary compost, and plant with the nose of each bulb protruding from the compost. Treat as hyacinths (page 54).

Propagation
It is not a practical proposition to propagate narcissi indoors.

SOME POPULAR SPECIES
Most of the varieties used for growing in pots are hybrids. Choose suitable varieties for indoor use (a good catalogue should suggest which). For very early flowering indoors two traditional varieties are 'Soleil d'Or' and 'Paper White', although some large-flowered daffodils are suitable. 'Paper White' is sometimes grown on a bowl of pebbles.

Neoregelia
PS/W/MH–HH

These bromeliads grow on the branches of jungle trees in their native habitat. Sometimes, at first sight, the leaves can be taken for the flower. The strap-shaped leaves grow as a rosette, and the centre ones become highly coloured when the plant flowers. The real flowers remain almost hidden inside the 'vase' formed by the leaves.

How to grow
Because bromeliads die after they flower (or at least the main plant dies; the offsets carry on and flower in due course), you cannot expect a neoregelia that you buy in flower to repeat the performance the next year. It will take several years for the offsets to flower, and they really need greenhouse conditions, so it may be best to discard the plant when it has lost its beauty. In the meantime just keep it watered with soft water, and top up the vase too. Mist the plant regularly.

Propagation
Not really sensible indoors—you will have to grow on the offsets for two or three years, providing high temperatures and humidity. And good light is needed to grow the plant on. If you do want to pot up the offsets, use a compost of three parts ericaceous mix to one part sharp sand.

SOME POPULAR SPECIES	
N. carolinae (Brazil) Broad, flat leaves, forming a spreading rosette. Normally green and glossy but central leaves assume a red colouring as flowering approaches.	**N. spectabilis** (Brazil) (Fingernail plant) Leathery, dark green leaves with white bands beneath. Each leaf is tipped with a large red spot.

Neoregelia carolinae 'Tricolor'

Nephrolepis
Ladder fern
PS/W/MH

Nephrolepis exaltata

A genus of about 30 ferns, found in tropical regions in all parts of the world. One species— *N. exaltata*—is very important commercially, large numbers being sold as houseplants. It is in fact one of the easier ferns for the home, though it still needs care.

How to grow
Few ferns will thrive and grow happily in the home, even with good attention, and this one is no exception. However, you can expect a reasonable life from it by keeping the compost evenly moist, feeding regularly with a weak feed (not full strength) and keeping it in a position of good indirect light.

Use soft water, and mist daily if possible. Daily misting is not essential, but the plant will last longer if you can give it this attention.

Propagation
Really a job for the professional (micropropagation is widely used commercially). The varieties do not come true from spores. Runners bearing young plants may appear, and these can be severed and potted up.

SOME POPULAR SPECIES	
N. exaltata (Tropics) Pinnate fronds sometimes over 60 cm (2 ft) long on a large specimen. There are several varieties with modified leaf form, such	as 'Teddy Junior' (crimped, wavy-edged leaflets), and 'Bostoniensis' (broad fronds) a variety known as the Boston fern.

Nertera
Bead plant
PS/C/MH

Nertera granadensis

About eight species occur in the wild, usually in mountain areas. Only one is grown as a house-plant and this is a diminutive plant grown for its berries, which are large for the size of the plant.

How to grow
The plant is usually bought when the berries have formed. Keep it in a cool place, then the berries will last longer.

It is worth trying to keep the plant after flowering. If you succeed it should flower about mid spring, when the temperature should be kept at about 13°C (55°F). It is a good idea to stand the plant outside for the summer, bringing it in when the berries colour.

To reduce the risk of rotting, water from beneath. Use soft water and keep the compost constantly moist during the summer.

Propagation
Divide a large plant in spring, repotting in a peat- or soil-based compost.

SOME POPULAR SPECIES	
N. granadensis *(N. depressa)* (South America, New Zealand, Australia) Forms a small clump clothed with small green	leaves, 4–6 mm (⅛–¼ in) across. The flowers are insignificant but these are followed by comparatively large orange-red berries.

Nidularium
PS/C/MH

A genus of 22 bromeliads native to Brazil, where they grow on rotting tree stumps and low tree branches in the rain forests. Although it is species such as *N. innocentii* that have tradition-ally represented them in cultivation, there are now hybrids available, such as *N. 'Citrinum'* (which has yellow 'flowers').

How to grow
Provide a light position, but out of direct sun, and ensure the compost does not dry out. Maintain a humid atmosphere, especially during the summer.

Nidularium

Propagation
Really something to undertake if you have a warm greenhouse where you can grow on the offsets for a couple of years once the parent plant dies (which it will do after flowering). Best regarded as an expendable houseplant.

SOME POPULAR SPECIES	
N. innocentii (Brazil) A rosette of strap-shaped leaves, purple-brown	overlaying the green upper surface; purple-red beneath.

Notocactus
FS–PS/C/MH–LH

Notocactus leninghausii

A genus of about 15 species that in nature grow mainly on rocky slopes. They are usually easy to grow, and flower prolifically—even from an early age. Because they do not mind warmth in winter, they are also easier than most to flower as a houseplant (a cold period is necessary to induce most cacti to flower).

How to grow
Unlike most cacti, the notocactus will tolerate some shade and winter warmth and still flower. Even so, keep it in a room that will not rise much above 10°C (50°F) in winter. During the summer, water whenever the compost starts to become dry, but in winter give only a little occasionally.

Feed occasionally during the summer. Repot young plants each spring, using a loam-based or cactus compost.

Propagation
Sometimes offsets are produced, which can be potted up after being allowed to dry for about a week. Usually, however, notocactus are propagated from seed.

SOME POPULAR SPECIES	
N. apricus (Uruguay) Light green stem with 15 to 20 notched, almost flattened ribs. Grey and reddish spines. Widely trumpet-shaped yellow flowers, up to 7.5 cm (3 in) long. **N. concinnus** (Brazil, Uruguay) A broadly globular green, glossy cactus, slightly depressed at the top. About 18 notched ribs with bristly yellow spines. Flowers up to 10 cm (4 in) long, yellow inside, red outside. **N. leninghausii** (Brazil) (Golden ball cactus) Cylindrical light green stems, usually forming clusters. About 20–30	ribs with fine, pale yellow spines. Flowers about 2.5 cm (1 in) across, lemon-yellow inside, green outside. Can be reluctant to flower. **N. mammulosus** (Argentina, Uruguay) Usually spherical stems with 18–20 deeply notched ribs. Yellow flowers with petals striped or flushed red outside. **N. ottonis** (Brazil, Argentina, Paraguay, Uruguay) Globular or cylindrical dark green stem, single or clump-forming. 10–12 rounded ribs with yellow-brown and red-brown spines. Yellow flowers, up to 10 cm (4 in) long.

Opuntia
Prickly pear
FS/C/MH–LH

Opuntias are many people's idea of a cactus: broad, flat pads, and hazardously spiny. There are over 200 species found all over the Americas. Some species have even become naturalised in the warmer parts of Europe.

How to grow
Make sure the plants receive plenty of sun during the summer. If you do not have a suitable sunny window, put them in a sheltered place, perhaps in a garden frame, outside. Keep cool in winter.

Water before the compost becomes dry in summer, and even in winter enough water should be given to prevent the compost drying out. Feed occasionally in summer.

When repotting, use a loam-based or cactus compost.

Propagation
Take cuttings. Detach pads or sections and let them dry for a day or two before inserting in the compost. If doing this in spring, use sections that have grown the previous year, if taking the cuttings in summer, use those that have grown earlier in the year.

Opuntia rufida

SOME POPULAR SPECIES	
O. macrodasys (Mexico) (Rabbit's ears, bunny ears) A branching, bushy cactus with pale green oval pads about 7.5–15 cm (3–6 in) long. Yellow flowers (rarely seen in cultivation). There are many varieties	of this cactus. **O. robusta** (Mexico) Almost circular blue-green pads up to 20 cm (8 in) or more across. **O. rufida** (Mexico) Yellow or orange flowers only on older plants.

Oxalis rubra

Oxalis
Wood sorrel
FS/C/MH

Anyone who has had oxalis as a weed in the garden may wonder why anyone should want to introduce it into their home. The species sometimes grown as pot-plants are quite innocuous, and although not ideal houseplants are pleasant short-term decorations.

In Continental Europe *O. deppei* is often given as a Christmas or New Year gift, because the foliage resembles a four-leafed clover, which is supposed to be lucky.

How to grow
Some bulb merchants offer the bulbs in the autumn. Pot them up, preferably in a loam-based compost, in small groups of four to six bulbs, about 5 cm (2 in) deep.

Water sparingly unless the temperature is very warm, and feed weekly while the plants are growing actively.

When the resting period approaches the foliage will wilt and die. Gradually withhold water until the compost is just prevented from becoming dust-dry. When growth starts again, resume normal watering.

The pots can be stood outside in summer.

Propagation
The bulbs will produce offsets, which provide a ready means of propagation.

SOME POPULAR SPECIES	
O. bowiei (*O. bowieana, O. purpurata bowiei*) (South Africa) Long-stalked, clover-like leaves. Pink flowers. **O. deppei** (Mexico) (Lucky clover) Bright	green, clover-like leaves with four lobes. The leaves fold up in the dark. Rose-red flowers. **O. rubra** (Mexico) Similar, but not as widely grown.

Pachystachys
Lollipop plant
PS–FS/W/HH

This is an attractive plant in flower, but not easy to keep. The curious upright cones of yellow-flowering bracts from which white flowers poke out, resemble the flowers of an aphelandra, and in shape also bear similarities to the shrimp plant *(Beloperone guttata)*.

How to grow
This plant needs plenty of warmth and humidity to do well. Mist daily. It will take full sun, and very good light will help to keep the plant compact. In spring, cut back the shoots a little; if conditions are right it should shoot again.

Feed fortnightly once new growth appears.

Young plants raised from cuttings, and best planted three to a pot, should have the growing tips pinched out a couple of times.

Propagation
Non-flowering shoots can be used as cuttings, in spring or summer.

SOME POPULAR SPECIES	
P. lutea (Mexico, Peru) Bright green, pointed oval leaves with conspicuous	veins. Upward-pointing bright yellow bracts with white flowers.

Pachystachys lutea

Parodia

FS/C/LH

There are about 40 species, native to Argentina, Bolivia, Brazil, and Paraguay. The genus is named after a Paraguayan botanist, Dr Parodi.

The species that you are likely to find in shops and garden centres should be easy to grow, and they are good cacti for beginners. They flower at an early age.

How to grow
Keep moderately moist in summer, dry in winter. Use soft water if possible. Feed once a month in summer.

When repotting use a loam-based or cactus compost.

Propagation
Because offsets are not produced freely, seed is the usual method of propagation. But this is tricky in the home, and expert growers may also graft the seedling on to another cactus.

SOME POPULAR SPECIES	
P. chrysacanthion (Argentina) Small, round cactus with spiralled ribs. Pale yellow thorns. Yellow flowers. **P. mairanana** A globular cactus with spiralled ribs. Apricot-coloured flowers in mide to late summer.	**P. microsperma** (Argentina) Small, round cactus, elongating with age. Numerous spiralled ribs. Orange or yellow flowers. **P. sanguiniflora** Small, spherical, spiralled ribs. Red flowers.

Parodia mairanana

Pelargonium

Geranium

FS/C/MH

Although 'geraniums' (a name that really belongs to a different group of plants) were used as houseplants long before the vast range that are now sold came on the scene, they are not ideal indoor plants. The bedding type of geranium (*P. zonale* and its derivatives) and the trailing ivy-leafed geranium (*P. peltatum* and its hybrids) are best regarded as summer bedding or greenhouse plants. Much better as houseplants are the Regal pelargoniums (*P. grandiflorum* hybrids) and the scented-leaved geraniums.

Pelargonium 'Decorator'

How to grow

Geraniums need sun to do well. And it will not be a disaster if the compost becomes dry occasionally (do not let this happen intentionally in summer). In winter they need very little water. Feed during the summer months and pinch out the shoot tips.

The overwintering temperature depends on the species, but the Regal and scented-leaved types described here need a minimum of about 7°C (45°F).

If you want large specimens, overwinter the complete Regal pelargonium plants, otherwise take cuttings in late summer and overwinter these.

Scented-leaved types are usually overwintered as they are, and they will tolerate a warm room, but will need shaping in spring. Repot at the same time if necessary.

Propagation

Cuttings taken in autumn or spring. The seed-raised geraniums do not usually make good houseplants.

SOME POPULAR SPECIES	
P. grandiflorum hybrids (Garden origin) (Regal, French, or Odier geraniums/pelargoniums) Ovate to palmate, toothed leaves. Flowers 4–6 cm (1½–2½ in) across in a range of colours, mainly pinks or purples, always with a darker blotch. **P. graveolens** (South Africa)	(Rose-scented geranium) Deeply divided leaves, edged white in the variety 'Variegatum'. Foliage fragrant when crushed. Flowers rose-red with violet patches on upper petals, but not the main feature. There are several other species with fragrant leaves which may also be variegated.

Pellaea

Button fern
PS/W/MH–LH

A large genus of ferns that grow mainly in dry areas of South America, South Africa, and New Zealand. They are unusual because most of these ferns grow in dry places such as on rocks.

How to grow

Unusual advice for a fern, but you do *not* need to mist the plant. Keep the compost moist but not wet. It is best watered from below. Feed fortnightly in summer.

The plant makes little root, so repotting is seldom necessary.

Propagation

From spores, or (much easier) by dividing an established plant.

SOME POPULAR SPECIES	
P. rotundifolia (New Zealand, Norfolk Island) Fronds with small, dark	green, round (hence the common name) to oval, leathery leaflets.

Pellaea rotundifolia

Peperomia
(smooth-leaved type)
PS–SH/H/MH

There are over 1,000 species in this genus, so it is not surprising that there are some useful house-plants among them. They grow mainly in the tropical and subtropical regions of America, which unfortunately means that they are not the easiest of houseplants to grow. The species described here have smooth, glossy leaves, those with wrinkled leaves are in the next entry.

How to grow
Avoid bright sunlight, but variegated species need a lighter position than green kinds if the variegation is not to suffer. Avoid overwatering, especially in winter. Feed monthly from spring to autumn.

Peperomias do well in a peat-based compost.

Propagation
Take stem cuttings, in spring or summer, at least 7.5 cm (3 in) long if possible.

SOME POPULAR SPECIES
P. clusiifolia (*P. obtusifolia clusiifolia*) (West Indies) Resembles *P. obtusifolia* but the leaves are more elongated and the margin is red. The variety 'Jeli' is attractively variegated green and pink. **P. obtusifolia** (*P. magnoliifolia*) (West Indies) (Desert privet) One of the most popular species, often used in mixed arrangements. Fleshy, glossy leaves about 5 cm (3 in) long, with cream or yellowish variegation in the variety 'Variegata' (the plain green species is seldom grown). There are varieties with more pronounced leaf markings, such as 'Green Gold' and 'USA'. This species is almost always sold under its previous name of *P. magnoliifolia*, which is also quite likely to be spelt *P. magnoliaefolia*.

Peperomia obtusifolia 'Variegata'

Peperomia
(wrinkled-leaved type)
PS–SH/H/MH

As explained in the previous entry, there are many species, and some of the plants are quite diverse in appearance. For that reason those with wrinkled leaves have been dealt with separately. Most peperomias are very useful for planting in bottle gardens or for adding to mixed arrangements of other plants with similar cultivation requirements.

Peperomia griseoargentea

How to grow

Avoid bright sunlight, but variegated species need a lighter position than green kinds if the variegation is not to suffer. Avoid overwatering, especially in winter. Feed monthly from spring to autumn.

Peperomias do well in a peat-based compost.

Propagation

The species listed are best propagated from leaf cuttings. Use newly matured leaves together with petiole, and insert the stalk into the compost.

SOME POPULAR SPECIES

P. caperata (Tropical America)
Heart-shaped, deeply corrugated leaves, dark green and about 2.5 cm (1 in) long. Leaf stalks and flowering stems pale pink. White, 'tail-like', upstanding flower spikes, held above the foliage.

P. griseoargentea *(P. hederifolia)* (Brazil)
Similar to the above species, but with larger leaves that are grey-green with darker green veins.
This species is most likely to be sold under the older name of *P. hederifolia.*

Pereskia

Barbados gooseberry
FS/W/MH–LH

These are interesting plants because they are non-succulent cacti. And although they have some spines the plants have leaves like most ordinary plants.

How to grow

Full sun will improve the colouring of the leaves. Water normally in summer, keep drier in winter, especially if the leaves fall. Feed fortnightly in summer.

Eventually pereskias make large sprawling plants which will need support.

Propagation

Half-ripe tip cuttings taken in summer may root. Alternatively sow seed in spring.

SOME POPULAR SPECIES

P. aculeata (Florida, West Indies, Mexico, Argentina)
A climbing shrub (though in a small specimen the climbing habit will not be noticeable), with oval to oblong leaves, pale green in the species, but olive green suffused with pink in the variety 'Godseffiana'. In the West Indies it is grown for its fruit (hence the common name of Barbados gooseberry).

Pereskia aculeata

Philodendron
(climbing type)
PS–SH/W/MH–HH

Philodendron scandens

The philodendrons are an important group of plants, both botanically (there are about 272 species) and as houseplants. Many of them make large, bold and striking plants for the right setting, but there are some easy species that will look right in any home, such as the sweetheart vine *(P. scandens)*. There are several hybrids sold under varietal names.

How to grow
Although the philodendrons described here will tolerate periods of poor light, they will do much better where the light is better (though not in direct sun). Variegated varieties in particular should be in good light.

Use soft water, preferably tepid, and keep the compost moist throughout the year, less so in winter of course.

A humid atmosphere is important; if you can mist the plants regularly they will be better for it. Cleaning the leaves also helps.

Feed fortnightly from spring to autumn. When repotting, use a peat-based compost.

Philodendrons are sometimes sold with a moss pole as support—this must be kept moist if it is to be worthwhile. Eventually the pole will be outgrown anyway and you will have to train the shoots up a convenient support, perhaps an indoor trellis or up a stairway.

Propagation
Take tip cuttings in spring or early summer. Pieces of stem with one to three joints can also be rooted as eye cuttings. Leggy plants can be air layered.

SOME POPULAR SPECIES

P. domesticum
(P. hastatum) (Brazil)
Moderately vigorous climber with dark green, entire leaves about 18 cm (7 in) long, similar to *P. erubescens,* but more arrow-shaped.
P. erubescens
(Colombia)
A vigorous climber rooting from each leaf joint. Arrowhead-shaped leaves about 23 cm (9 in) long, dark glossy green with copper or purple sheen. Leaf stalks and stems greenish-red or purple. There are several varieties, usually with redder or greener leaves.
P. laciniatum
(Venezuela, Brazil)
The leaves, held out on slender stalks, are deeply

incised almost into a palmate appearance.
P. melanochrysum
(Colombia)
A climber with dark green, velvety and white-veined arrow-shaped leaves that hang down so that the stems are almost hidden. It may be listed as *P. melanochryson*
P. panduriforme (Brazil)
Arrowhead-shaped leaves about 23 cm (9 in) long.
P. scandens (Panama) (Sweetheart vine) Heart-shaped mid to dark green, leathery leaves, about 10 cm (4 in) long, with slender points. The most widely grown species, and one of the easiest. A useful trailer, and suitable for a hanging pot.

Philodendron

(bushy type)
PS–SH/W/MH–HH

Some of the climbing species used as house-plants have been described in the previous entry.

How to grow
As previous species, though there will be no problem of what to do with the climbing stems.

Propagation
Division (you may have to remove the growing point in early summer, then wait a year for lateral shoots to grow at the base). Seed is an alternative, though more practical if you have a warm green-house.

Top right Philodendron bipinnatifidum

SOME POPULAR SPECIES	
P. bipinnatifidum (Brazil) A compact plant with lobed and deeply incised green leaves that arise from a central growing point, on long stalks.	**P. selloum** (Brazil) Large heart-shaped bright green leaves, up to 75 cm (30 in) long, the margins incised all round. These arise from the base of the plant on long stalks.

Phoenix

Date palm
PS–FS/C/MH–HH

The true date palm, *P. dactylifera*, is similar to the species described below, but *P. canariensis* and *P. roebelenii* are the ones generally used as house-plants.

Phoenix canariensis

How to grow
Once the plants reach three or four years old, they will take all the sun you can give them, but younger plants are best provided with shade from strong sun. *P. roebelenii* will need frequent misting, but *P. canariensis* is less demanding.

In winter, water only when the surface of the compost appears dry. Feed fortnightly from spring to autumn.

Repot small plants each spring, using a loam-based compost. Just topdress old plants in large pots.

Propagation
Normally raised from seed, but this is a slow job and not an easy task in the home. *P. roebelenii* can sometimes be divided.

SOME POPULAR SPECIES	
P. canariensis (Canary Islands) (Canary Island date palm) A chunky-looking plant with dark green fronds, upright at first then arching. Forms a thick stem.	**P. roebelenii** (East Asia) (Pygmy date palm) An almost stemless plant, the fronds reaching about 60 cm (2 ft). Much more suitable size and shape than the previous species as a houseplant.

Pilea

PS/W/HH–MH

Pilea cadierei

The pileas give us some popular foliage plants, although they tend to deteriorate quite rapidly indoors. The fact that they are nevertheless popular is testimony to their visual appeal.

How to grow

Good light is essential for the larger-leaved kinds if they are not to become leggy. High humidity is also important if they are to do well.

Water freely in summer, much more sparingly in winter. Feed fortnightly from spring to autumn.

P. cadierei will become leggy and untidy unless the growing points are pinched out in spring to encourage bushiness.

Propagation

Cuttings root easily. Late spring or summer is the best time.

SOME POPULAR SPECIES
P. cadierei (Vietnam) (Aluminium plant) Opposite, oblong to oval leaves, dark green with silvery sunken marks. **P. involucrata** *(P. pubescens)* (Tropical America) (Friendship plant) Oval, deeply quilted leaves with pale green margins. **P. microphylla** *(P. muscosa)* (Tropical America) (Artillery plant, gunpowder plant) Tiny leaves in opposite pairs, giving the much-branched plant a ferny look. The yellowish-green flowers expel puffs of pollen (hence the common names). **P. spruceana** (Peru, Venezuela) Oval, wrinkled and quilted bronze leaves with silvery bands running the length of the leaf (in the variety 'Norfolk') or just a central silver stripe ('Silver Tree').

Plectranthus

PS–FS/W/MH

These plants are rather neglected commercially, but they are not difficult to grow and will tolerate a reasonable degree of neglect (though obviously they grow better with good care). The trailing species are perhaps best displayed in a hanging pot. It is usual to grow about three plants in a pot, to provide all-round coverage.

How to grow

P. oertendahlii should be protected from full sun in summer, but the other species listed will not mind.

Plectranthus coleoides 'Marginatus'

Water generously in summer. Feeding is not normally necessary. Repot each spring using a peat or soil-based compost.

Pinch out the tips of shoots regularly to encourage bushiness.

It may be necessary to trim back the growth on old plants to keep them within bounds. Cuttings root easily if you want to maintain a supply of fresh young plants.

Propagation
Tip cuttings root very easily, even in water.

SOME POPULAR SPECIES

P. coleoides 'Marginatus' Height and spread about 30 cm (1 ft) when pot grown. Leaves have clear white margins.
P. oertendahlii (South Africa)
A creeping plant, rooting easily at the nodes. Leaves almost circular, about 5 cm (2 in) across, with silver veins.
P. parviflorus *(P. australis)* (Australia) Another creeping and trailing species, useful for a basket or hanging pot. The leaves are green, with no variegation.

Polyscias
PS/W/HH

Neglected plants in Britain, now becoming more popular. They have an upright, sometimes rather lanky habit, that is not to everyone's taste, and the yellow variegation of some plants can make the leaves look diseased. Despite that, they can make striking plants. Some are raised commercially from imported pieces of stem that are then rooted, rather like some yuccas and dracaenas.

Pinch out the growing tips of plants raised from cuttings a few times, to encourage bushiness.

How to grow
Frequent misting is one of the keys to success. Use soft water for this and for moistening the compost. Feed fortnightly in spring and summer.

Use an ericaceous compost when repotting.

Propagation
Take cuttings in spring, but ensure there is a piece of main stem too, not just the stalk of a compound leaf.

SOME POPULAR SPECIES

P. balfouriana *(Aralia balfouriana)* (New Caledonia)
Compound leaves usually with three leaflets, though single leaves occur. Green, round, with serrated edge. Some varieties have grey or yellowish green markings, especially along the veins or around the leaf margins.

Polyscias balfouriana

Primula

PS/C/MH

Primulas are a large group of plants—there are over 500 species, and range from hardy to tender. Most of them are especially useful because they flower early. Primula comes from the word *primus* meaning the first.

There are two main groups used as house-plants: the tender species such as *P. obconica* and *P. malacoides*, and the hardy primulas *P. vulgaris* (primrose) and *P. elatior* hybrids (polyanthus). You used to be able to tell the last two apart by the fact that polyanthus bear several flowers on a single stalk carried well clear of the leaves. The modern varieties have been cross-bred to such an extent that now some of the polyanthus type flower close to the crown and it can be easy to mistake the two at first glance.

How to grow

Hardy species Bring into the house as they come into flower (the stage at which they are usually bought), and keep in a cool room to extend the flowering period. Do not let them dry out. Remove dead flowers. Once flowering has finished they are finished as houseplants . . . but there is use in them yet. Plant them in the garden. They should flower in future years.

Tender species These are best regarded as short-term houseplants, and discarded after flowering unless you have a greenhouse.

They are usually bought in flower and will last better in a cool room. Keep the compost moist but not waterlogged. Remove dead flowers. If the plant is to be retained, use soft water.

If you want to keep the plant, repot after flowering, and begin to feed next time the plant starts to come into flower. It is usually better to use a fresh plant each year, however.

Propagation

From seed, but not really a practical proposition indoors. If you do not have a greenhouse for raising seedlings, buy the plants. It is not worth trying to divide old plants.

SOME POPULAR SPECIES

P. elatior hybrids *(P. polyantha)* (Garden origin) (Polyanthus) Hardy. Flowers up to 4 cm (1½ in) across, in clusters carried above the rosette-like spread of low-lying leaves. Various colours, usually with contrasting eye. The nomenclature of these plants is confused. The polyanthus is the result of crosses between several species. It is often listed as *P. polyantha*.

P. x kewensis (Garden hybrid) Tender. Light green, spatula-shaped, toothed leaves, often covered with a waxy white farina (powder). Yellow flowers in whorls one above the other.

P. malacoides (China) (Fairy primrose) Tender. Pale green oval leaves, topped with 12 mm (½ in) flowers arranged in tiers along a slender stem. Colours usually pale lilac to red.

P. obconica (China) Tender. Light green, oval, slightly hairy leaves. Clusters of 2.5 cm (1 in) flowers. Colours include pink, red, lilac, or blue.

The plant will cause a rash if handled by anyone allergic to it. Some strains have much less of the chemical that causes the problem (it may even be absent).

P. vulgaris hybrids *(P. acaulis)* (Western and Southern Europe) (Primrose) Hardy. The hybrids grown as pot plants are much bolder and more colourful than the wild primrose.

Rosette of bright green, spreading leaves, on top of which nestle flowers on individual stalks arising from the crown. Colours include yellow, red, and blue and purple shades, many with contrasting eye.

Primula obconica

Pteris

PS–SH/W/HH

A large and important genus of over 250 ferns. Some species are widely available as house-plants, though the chances of keeping them indoors long-term are not good unless you give them exceptional care. In nature they grow in humid forests. In some hybrids the leaf fronds are attractively variegated, or much divided and 'crested' at the tips as shown in *P. c.* 'whimsettii'.

How to grow

Daily misting will be worthwhile. They are also likely to do better arranged in a group, where the humidity is likely to be higher. Avoid hot, dry air, such as by a radiator.

The compost must never dry out, and plenty of water will be needed in summer. Use soft water. Feed weekly (at half strength) from spring to autumn and repot only when necessary using a peat-based compost.

Propagation

As you are only likely to need a few extra plants, division in spring is the easiest method. Spores are an alternative, but much more difficult.

SOME POPULAR SPECIES

P. cretica (Tropics and subtropics)
(Ribbon fern) Pale green, leathery fronds divided into two to six strap-shaped pinnae on either side of the midrib. There are many varieties, one of the most widely available being 'Albolineata' (white stripe along centre of each pinna).
P. ensiformis (India, China to Australia)
Similar to the above species, but more delicate and slender, with more elongated pinnae. It is usually grown in a variegated form, such as 'Victoriae' (silvery marks along veins) and 'Evergemiensis' (similar to the previous variety but more boldly marked).
P. tremula (New Zealand, Australia)
(Australian bracken, Australian brake) A delicate-looking fern with feathery fronds, not unlike large carrot foliage.

Top *Pteris cretica* 'Whimsettii'
Bottom *P. c.* 'Albolineata'

Rebutia
Crown cactus
FS/C/MH

A genus generally free-flowering small, globular cacti, named after a M. P. Rebut, a Paris cactus dealer. They grow wild in Argentina and Bolivia. They flower young, which makes them understandably popular.

How to grow
A warm sunny summer and a cool winter are the best way to get these cacti to flower. Keep the plants dry from late autumn until spring when the buds become visible, then start watering again.

Propagation
Remove offshoots produced at the base, and root in a sandy compost. Seed germinates easily.

Rebutia

SOME POPULAR SPECIES	
R. chrysacantha (Argentina) Grows to about 6 cm (2½ in) high. Golden spines and red flowers up to 5 cm (2 in) across. **R. marsoneri** (Argentina) Dark green, broad, flattened stem, depressed at crown. Yellow flowers up to 4 cm (1½ in) across. **R. minuscula** (Argentina)	A flattened sphere. Red flowers up to 4 cm (1½ in) across. **R. pygmaea** (Bolivia) Oval, olive green to grey body. Purple flowers about 2.5 cm (1 in) across. **R. xanthocarpa** (Argentina) Clump-forming. Pale green stems covered with white spines. Red flowers.

Rhipsalidopsis
Easter cactus
PS/C–W/HH–MH

These forest cacti grow as epiphytes in the tropical forests of Brazil. Although ungainly plants out of flower, they justify being grown once they burst into bloom in spring. And they are easy to grow and flower.

How to grow
The key to flowering success is to keep them cool in the winter (ideally in the range 10–15°C/ 50–59°F), although to some extent it is a combination of day length and temperature that

Rhipsalidopsis gaertneri

determines the actual time of flowering.

Repot after flowering, using a lime-free compost. If you find them unattractive out of flower, stand them in a sheltered, partly shaded spot outdoors for the summer, and bring inside again in the autumn well before there is any likelihood of frost.

Water freely during the growing period, but only give just enough water to prevent the compost drying out completely while the plants are resting in the autumn and winter. The plants should not be allowed to shrivel.

Misting is not essential, but they will be much better for it.

Propagation

Tip segments can be used as cuttings in late spring (let them dry off for a day or two before inserting in the compost). Seed is not a practical proposition for raising indoors.

SOME POPULAR SPECIES	
R. gaertneri *(Schlumbergera gaertneri)* (Brazil) Flattened or angled, arching, jointed stems that	serve as leaves. Bold, bright scarlet flowers with long, pointed overlapping petals, about 5 cm (2 in) across.

Rhoeo

Boat lily, Moses-in-the-crib
PS/W/MH

There is only one species *R. spathacea* (though it is more likely to be sold as *R. discolor*), native to Central America. The common names reflect the boat-shaped purple bracts that nestle at the base of the leaves and hold the inconspicuous white flowers.

How to grow

Water normally from spring to autumn, and never let the compost dry out even in winter. Feed fortnightly from spring to autumn. Repot in spring.

Propagation

Cuttings (though to stimulate enough sideshoots you may have to remove the top of the plant). If offsets are produced at the base these can be potted up. Leggy plants can be air layered.

SOME POPULAR SPECIES	
R. spathacea *(R. discolor)* (Central America) Semi-erect strap-shaped leaves up to 30 cm (1 ft) long, dark green on top,	purple beneath. The variety 'Vittata' has yellow stripes running lengthwise along the leaves.

Rhoeo spathacea 'Vittata'

Rhoicissus

PS–SH/W/MH

The botanists have been at work on this genus, and the species that you may well be looking for under this name, *R. rhomboidea,* is now classified as *Cissus rhombifolia.* It is still, however, usually sold as a rhoicissus and we have included it under that name.

How to grow
Although poor light is tolerated, best results are likely to be achieved in a reasonably well lit position, that is not too hot. In a warm, centrally-heated room in winter, the leaves will benefit from regular misting. Water generously and feed fortnightly in summer.

R. rhomboidea will make a cascading plant and is suitable for a hanging basket (the basket must be in good light if it is not to disappoint).

Propagation
Eye cuttings or tip cuttings. The rooted cuttings are usually potted three to a pot.

SOME POPULAR SPECIES	
R. capensis (South Africa) Climber with almost heart-shaped emerald green leaves, up to 15 cm (6 in) across. Brown and felty underneath. **R. rhomboidea** *(Cissus rhombifolia)* (Central and	South America) (Grape ivy) Dark green glossy leaves divided into three leaflets on short stalks. In the variety 'Ellen Danica' (a superior form) these are deeply toothed. Climbs by tendrils.

Rhoicissus rhomboidea 'Ellen Danica'

Rosa

Rose

FS/C/MH

Roses are not indoor plants, and although miniatures can be used to provide interest for a few weeks, the plants will gradually deteriorate unless put outside. They are therefore best regarded as short-term plants for the home, with the bonus of providing long-term garden interest afterwards.

How to grow
Plenty of light and a cool room are the best way to keep the plant flowering if you intend to plant it out afterwards.

If you want to keep it as a pot-plant, plunge the pot in the ground outdoors after flowering, and

prune in spring as you would a normal rose. Bring the plant indoors when the flowers are forming.

Propagation
Cuttings rooted outdoors. Seed is sometimes sold, but results can be variable, and it is not a good idea to attempt to raise them from seed in the home. Commercially they may be grafted.

SOME POPULAR SPECIES	
R. chinensis 'Minima' *(R. roulettii)* (China) The miniature roses sold now are hybrids. They	resemble large roses (there are singles and doubles), but are miniature in all their parts.

Rosa 'Anna Ford'

Saintpaulia
African violet
PS/H/HH

One of the most popular houseplants, but one that needs care if it is not to deteriorate in home conditions. It was named in honour of Baron Walter von Saint Paul-Illaire, a German who discovered *S. ionantha* while serving in East Africa. It is a native of the Usambara mountains.

How to grow
Try to make the air as humid as possible, but avoid spraying the leaves (they are hairy and the water may collect on them and cause disfigurement). Avoid wetting the leaves when watering, which should be done with soft water. Never let the compost become waterlogged: overwatering is a common cause of failure.

Direct sunlight is not a good idea, but saintpaulias do need plenty of good light to develop flower buds. Long days are also needed to encourage flowering. Commercially, year-round flowering can be achieved by artificial lighting.

Feed monthly while they are growing actively. Repot each spring, although cuttings root so easily that it is worth keeping a supply of fresh plants coming along so that you can discard the old one.

Saintpaulia ionantha

Propagation
Leaf petiole cuttings root easily. Old plants can be divided. Can be raised from seed, but this really needs a greenhouse.

SOME POPULAR SPECIES	
S. ionantha (Central Africa) Deep green heart-shaped leaves arising from a crown on relatively long stalks. Single or double flowers (some fringed),	mainly in shades of purple or pink, produced in loose clusters held clear of the leaves. There are many varieties, which are partly the result of crossing with other species.

Sansevieria

Mother-in-law's tongue
FS/C–W/LH

These desert plants grow in places like Ethiopia, and consequently are tolerant of dry roots if you forget to water, and will take full sun (not many houseplants will). As they are also attractive they have many merits as houseplants.

How to grow
Avoid waterlogged compost. Make sure any water that you apply can drain away freely. Feed monthly in summer.

Only repot when the roots are about to burst out of the pot—sansevierias actually do well in pots small for the size of plant (but you will need a clay pot and a loam-based compost to counterbalance the heavy top growth).

Propagation
Divide established plants. The green species can be propagated from leaf cuttings (make 5 cm/2 in sections across the leaf). Variegated varieties will not produce variegated plants from this type of cutting.

Sansevieria trifasciata 'Laurentii'

SOME POPULAR SPECIES	
S. trifasciata (West Africa) Sword-like, thick, fleshy, leaves up to 1.5 m (5 ft) long on a mature plant. Dull green with mottled grey cross-banding. The more decorative variety 'Laurentii' has creamy-	yellow leaf margins. Different in form is the variety 'Hahnii' (sometimes listed as a species, *S. hahnii*), which forms a rosette only 15 cm (6 in) high, and a gold-edged version of this called 'Golden Hahnii'.

Sauromatum

Monarch of the East/voodoo lily
PS/C/MH

The species sold as a houseplant is really an oddity. It is sold as a dry bulb (try bulb catalogues), which will flower without being planted in compost. An arum-like inflorescence is produced, which is unusual rather than attractive. The flowers have an unpleasant smell. The leaves that follow are quite handsome.

How to grow
If you want to flower the plant as a dry bulb, there

is nothing much to do except leave it to flower. A saucer of sand will help to keep it stable.

The plant is usually discarded once it has flowered and you have had the benefit of its foliage. If you want to enjoy the leaves, you will need to pot up the bulb for stability.

You could plant the bulb outdoors in a sheltered position after flowering. In mild areas it should survive for future years, otherwise you can lift it and bring it indoors for the winter.

Propagation
Not practical in the home.

SOME POPULAR SPECIES	
S. venosum *(S. guttatum)* (Central Asia) Arum-like flower, with long, purple-spotted spathe, from which an	upright 'tail' stands erect. After flowering, attractive spotted stems emerge, topped with large palmate leaves.

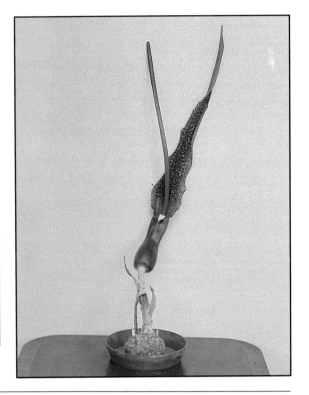

Sauromatum venosum

Saxifraga
Mother of thousands
PS/C–W/MH

Saxifrages are usually thought of as rock plants, but the species described here is a common houseplant. Although not reliably hardy, it is a tough plant and the green type will usually survive planted out in the garden.

How to grow
A cool, light, airy environment is likely to give the best results. The variegated forms need more warmth. Be careful not to overwater in winter. Feed fortnightly in summer.

If planting in a hanging basket or pot, make sure it is in a light position. If you hang it near the top of a window light may not be as good as you think.

Propagation
Very easy. Pot up the little plantlets that form on the trailing stems.

SOME POPULAR SPECIES	
S. stolonifera *(S. sarmentosa)* (China, Japan) Roundish leaves with silver veins on the upper surface. The variety 'Tricolor' has pale yellow	and pink variegation, but is less robust, and needs more warmth than the green form. Long, trailing runners, on which small plants develop.

Saxifraga stolonifera 'Tricolor'

Schefflera
PS/W/MH

A genus of trees and shrubs named in honour of
J. C. Scheffler, an 18th-century Danzig botanist
and friend of Linnaeus. The two species grown
as houseplants are attractive for their habit and
overall shape rather than the beauty of individual
leaves, which are plain green. Although they have
long been popular in New Zealand, they have
only become widely grown in the USA and
Britain in recent years.

How to grow
Water moderately in summer, a little less in
winter. Feed monthly from spring to autumn.

Repot annually in spring.

Keep in a light position in winter. Avoid the
combination of high temperature and low light
level.

Propagation
Seed is one method used commercially, but the
plants can be variable. Cuttings are better in the
home, but are not easy to root.

SOME POPULAR SPECIES	
S. actinophylla *(Brassaia actinophylla)* (Australia) As a pot-plant it forms a single stem with radiating glossy green palmately divided leaves. **S. arboricola** *(Heptapleurum arboricola)* (South East Asia) (Parasol plant) Glossy	green leaves arranged finger-like on slender stalks, elegantly held away from the central stem. There are various varieties, including 'Variegata', which has yellow and green leaves. This species is frequently sold as heptapleurum.

Schefflera actinophylla

Schlumbergera
Christmas cactus
PS/W/MH

This popular cactus has been the victim of
several name changes. You are just as likely to
find the Christmas cactus sold as *Zygocactus
truncatus*. In fact the plants grown are mainly
hybrids anyway.

How to grow
The plant can spend the summer in the garden,
keeping it well watered and fed fortnightly, but it
should be brought in before the weather turns
cold. Once indoors, keep it cool and dry until the

Schlumbergera truncata

pink buds appear. Try to make sure that the plant is not subject to artificial light at this time, otherwise flowering may be upset.

Once the buds are forming, water moderately, and do not turn the plant (the buds may drop).

Propagation
Take cuttings of the jointed segments in summer (let them dry for a few days before inserting in the compost).

SOME POPULAR SPECIES	
S. x buckleyi (Garden hybrid) Jointed, flattened stems that serve as leaves. Flowers usually magenta or rose, 5–7.5 cm (2–3 in) long, in winter.	**S. truncata** *(Zygocactus truncatus)* (Brazil) Similar to above. There are many named varieties, though most are hybrids anyway. Colours include crimson, lilac, purple.

Scindapsus aureus

Scindapsus
Devil's ivy
PS–SH/W/MH–LH

A group of evergreen climbers related to philodendrons. The species that is most grown as a houseplant *(S. aureus)* has been moved around by botanists and you may now find it in technical books under the names *Rhaphidophora aurea* or *Epipremnum aureum*. Scindapsus is the name under which you will amost certainly find it sold.

Use as a climber (perhaps up a moss pole) or trailer (maybe in a hanging pot).

How to grow
An easy houseplant. Keep the compost moist in summer, but in winter reduce the amount of water as the temperature drops. Feed fortnightly from spring to autumn.

Use a lime-free compost when repotting.

Propagation
Take cuttings of tips or basal shoots in early summer. Leaf-bud cuttings are also possible, but probably more trouble if you want only a few plants.

SOME POPULAR SPECIES	
S. aureus *(Rhaphidophora aurea, Epipremnum aureum)* (Solomon Islands) Climber producing aerial roots. Oval, pointed, glossy leaves about 10 cm (4 in) long, bright green suffused yellow.	'Marble Queen' has less green and is heavily dappled with white; 'Golden Queen' has almost entirely yellow leaves. These varieties are more difficult to grow than the species.

Sedum
Stonecrop
FS/C/LH

Sedum rubrotinctum

This is a large genus of over 500 species, most of them plants for the rock garden. A few make interesting houseplants.

How to grow
Although *S. sieboldii* can be watered normally during the summer (it dies down for the winter), the other sedums listed below should be given a little water at any time. Feeding should not be necessary if you repot the plants each spring.

Avoid too much warmth in winter, otherwise they may lose some of their colouring.

A loam-based compost is likely to suit them best.

Propagation
Sedums can be raised from seed, but for just a few plants cuttings are a better method. Species with large fleshy leaves, such as *S. pachyphyllum*, can be rooted from leaf cuttings (let them dry off for a week before inserting in compost).

SOME POPULAR SPECIES
S. lineare 'Variegatum' (China, Japan) Small, grey-green linear leaves edged white, arranged in threes on pinkish trailing stems. **S. pachyphyllum** (Mexico) Succulent, club-shaped to cylindrical blue-green leaves tipped red (the German common name for this plant is *Schnapsnase*—loosely translated a drinker's nose). Upright, branching shape. Yellow flowers in dense clusters a couple of inches across. **S. rubrotinctum** (Mexico) Base-branching habit with thin, erect stems. Fleshy, cylindrical leaves, green becoming red-brown in strong sunshine or drought. The variety 'Aurora' has grey-green leaves tinged pink to salmon. Yellow flowers. **S. sieboldii** (Japan) A distinctive sedum—its bluish-green leaves are flat, and it tends to shed them in the autumn, fresh shoots and leaves appearing in spring. The variety usually grown is 'Mediovariegatum', which has a white blotch in the centre of each leaf. In strong sunlight the leaves take on a reddish hue.

Selaginella
PS/W–H/HH

The selaginellas look rather like large mosses. Many of them grow wild in tropical rain forests. They do not like it in a typical living-room. If you want them to last, be prepared to give them the right environment (a bottle garden is ideal).

How to grow
Maintain at least 15°C (60°F), above if possible, and high humidity. If you do not grow them in an enclosed environment such as in a bottle or under a glass dome, mist them daily.

Never let the compost dry out. Give them a foliar feed occasionally during the summer.

A peat-based compost should suit them when repotting, which is done in spring.

Propagation

Division—an easy job because in a humid environment shoots will send out roots into the compost anyway. Cut off any suitable shoot tips and insert them in a mixture of peat and sand, preferably in a propagator.

<table>
<tr><td colspan="2" align="center">SOME POPULAR SPECIES</td></tr>
<tr><td>

S. apoda (North America) Pale green, finely toothed foliage, forming a low mound.
S. kraussiana (South Africa)
(Spreading club moss) Creeping stems, leaves much divided. 'Aurea' is

</td><td>

especially attractive because of its yellow colour.
S. martensii (Mexico) An upright, 'tufty' habit; coarser appearance than previous species. The tips of 'Watsoniana' are silvery-white.

</td></tr>
</table>

Selaginella spp.

Sempervivum
Houseleek
FS/C/LH

These interesting plants seem to be able to cling to an existence in the most unlikely places—old roofs, dry walls, and rocks. They do flower, but most are grown for the attractive rosettes of leaves. The species below are only representative—you could collect a vast number of species and hybrids.

How to grow

There isn't much to do. They almost thrive on neglect. No need to feed. Water needed only occasionally. Just provide good light.

Propagation

The plants produce offsets around the parent plant. Simply detach rooted offsets.

<table>
<tr><td colspan="2" align="center">SOME POPULAR SPECIES</td></tr>
<tr><td>

S. arachnoideum (Europe, Pyrenees) (Cobweb houseleek) Globular rosettes 2.5– 4 cm (1–1½ in) across. The green leaves may be flushed red, and the tips are covered with a cobweb-like mat of hairs.

</td><td>

Rose-red flowers on 15 cm (6 in) stems.
S. tectorum (Pyrenees, Alps)
Rosette of bright green leaves tipped chestnut-brown. Pink flowers. There are many hybrids. Height 2.5–5 cm (1–2 in).

</td></tr>
</table>

Sempervivum

Setcreasea
Purple heart
FS–PS/C/MH

The species most used as a houseplant—*S. pallida*, just as likely to be found as *S. purpurea*—would make a nice houseplant if only it did not become so straggly indoors. You need to be prepared to keep the plant in good light, and to pinch back any ungainly growth, to make the most of an otherwise pretty plant.

How to grow
Keep moist in summer, fairly dry in winter. Feed occasionally in summer. Give it a light position if possible.

Repot in spring. But it is a good idea to replace with fresh plants regularly. Propagation is easy.

Propagation
Take cuttings, preferably in spring.

SOME POPULAR SPECIES	
S. pallida *(S. purpurea)* (Mexico) Erect, oblong to lance-	shaped purple leaves. Stems also purple. Small rose-purple flowers.

Setcreasea purpurea

Smithiantha
Temple bells
PS/H/HH

These rhizomatous herbaceous plants with fox-glove-like flowers are not widely sold as pot-plants in flower, but the rhizomes can be bought from most bulb merchants and mail-order seedsmen.

How to grow
Plant the rhizomes in moist peat at about 21°C (70°F) until they start to shoot. Then pot them up in groups of three or five to a 12.5 cm (5 in) pot. They will then be better in a greenhouse until they come into flower, otherwise keep them in a

Smithiantha

light position though not in full sun.

Keep the compost moist throughout the summer, and feed fortnightly, reducing the amount when the plants have finished flowering. Overwinter the rhizomes indoors, in the compost. Repot in spring, preferably in a peat-based compost.

Propagation
Divide old rhizomes once they have formed

shoots. Each section needs at least one shoot. Leaf cuttings can be taken in early summer.

SOME POPULAR SPECIES
Smithiantha hybrids are the plants usually grown. Nodding, foxglove-like flowers carried in clusters above velvety, heart- shaped leaves. Colours include pink, yellow, orange, red and cream, often flushed or marked with a second colour.

Solanum

Winter cherry/Christmas cherry/ Jerusalem cherry
PS/C/MH

These popular winter-interest plants are grown for their orange berries. They may contain a poison (the true species does, but the plants now sold have a mixed parentage and these berries may not be so toxic), which is actually more of a hazard when the berries are still green. It is best to avoid this plant if you have small children likely to be tempted by the attractive fruit.

How to grow
Unless you have a greenhouse it is best to buy the plant in berry and discard it afterwards. To keep the berries on for as long as possible, keep the plant in a cool room, in good light, and mist the plant occasionally.

To try to keep the plant for another year, keep the compost moist, the air humid, and repot in spring after cutting back all growth by about one-third. Then place the plant outdoors for the summer, bringing it back indoors before the nights get cold. The flowers (which appear in early summer) will not set a good crop of berries if the plant is underwatered or overwatered at that time. If you neglect watering during the summer, leaves will probably drop too.

Propagation
Usually raised from seed, although this is not a good method if you do not have a greenhouse. You could take cuttings.

SOME POPULAR SPECIES
S. pseudocapsicum *(S. capsicastrum)* (Brazil) Winter cherry, Jerusalem cherry, Christmas cherry. These may be listed as distinct species. The plants we grow are derived from these, and possibly other, species. Grown for their orange to red round berries, sometimes more than 12 mm (½ in) across. The small, white flowers are insignificant. There are many varieties, but the varietal name is unlikely to be mentioned on the label.

Solanum capsicastrum

Sparmannia
African hemp/house lime
PS/C/MH

Sparmannia africana

A genus of seven species, named after Andreas Sparmann, a Swedish botanist. Only one species is in general cultivation, and this can be used as a houseplant while it is young. It is grown mainly as a foliage plant; although it may flower the blooms are not very striking.

How to grow
Give just sufficient water to prevent drying out in winter, but water generously from spring till autumn. Feed weekly during the summer. Although they should not be in direct summer sun through the window, provide a light position.

This is a fast-growing plant and it is sensible to start afresh each year. But if you want to keep it, repot the plant in spring after flowering. It can stand in a sheltered and fairly shady spot outside for the summer. In early summer, cut the plant back to about 30 cm (1 ft)—it will soon make a lot of fresh growth.

Propagation
Take cuttings in spring. Once rooted and growing, pinch out the growing tip to encourage bushiness.

SOME POPULAR SPECIES	
S. africana (South Africa) Heart-shaped, bright green leaves about 15–20 cm (6–8 in) long, covered with soft hairs.	White flowers with prominent stamens, 2.5–4 cm (1–1½ in) across.

Spathiphyllum
Peace lily
PS/W/HH

These plants are not unlike a white anthurium (page 10); they are easier to grow, but still not beginners' plants.

How to grow
The key to success is to provide a very humid atmosphere, although it is less demanding in this respect during the resting period from mid autumn to mid winter.

Spathiphyllum wallisii

Water generously in summer, using tepid water, only moderately in winter when the plant is resting. Feed fortnightly in summer. Cleaning the leaves with a damp sponge improves the appearance.

Propagation

Divide established plants when repotting, which is usually done in spring.

SOME POPULAR SPECIES	
S. floribundum (Colombia) Dark green, oval leaves. The white spathe is about 11 cm (4½ in) long.	**S. x 'Mauna Loa'** Similar to the above, but with larger 'flowers'. **S. wallisii** (Colombia) Similar to *S. floribundum*.

Stephanotis
Wax flower/Madagascar jasmine
PS/W/MH

The stephanotis that we use as a houseplant will make a large climber in a greenhouse. Fortunately it is usually sold with its climbing vine trained around a wire hoop. Commercial growers can get the plants into flower at various times of the year by adjusting the day length and interrupting the night with periods of illumination. You will not really be able to achieve this in the home, so in future years the plant is likely to flower in summer.

How to grow

You may find that some buds drop if the plant is reorientated. Try to move its position as little as possible once it is coming into flower. Train new tendrils around the wire hoop.

Water freely in summer (soft water is preferable), reducing the amount in winter. Keep in a fairly cool room for the winter—not over 15°C (60°F). If kept too warm it will probably become spindly.

Repot young plants annually in spring. Older plants will need repotting less frequently.

Propagation

Take cuttings from the previous year's wood, in spring or summer. A propagator will help.

SOME POPULAR SPECIES	
S. floribunda (Madagascar) An evergreen twining or trailing plant with oval,	glossy, green leaves. Clusters of star-like white, waxy-looking, fragrant flowers.

Stephanotis floribunda

Syngonium
Goosefoot plant
PS–SH/W–H/MH

These plants resemble some of the philodendrons in leaf shape and climbing habit. They are sometimes grown up a moss pole, or allowed to trail from a hanging pot. You could also try growing them as epiphytes if you want to add variety to a bromeliad tree.

The shape of the leaves changes with time. As the plant becomes larger the leaves usually have more lobes.

How to grow
Use soft water. The compost should not be over-watered, so keep only moderately moist in summer. Misting the leaves occasionally will be beneficial. Feed fortnightly when the plants are growing actively. Repot each spring, preferably in a peat-based compost.

Propagation
Tip cuttings or eye cuttings can be used. Leggy plants can be air layered.

Syngonium podophyllum 'Imperial White'

SOME POPULAR SPECIES	
S. podophyllum (Central America) Leaf shape variable. Arrowhead-shaped to as many as 11 lobes. 'Albolineatum' has leaf veins lined with white or	cream. 'Emerald Gem' has silver-white variegation. The plant is sometimes known as nephthytis in the USA.

Thunbergia
Black-eyed Susan
FS/(W)/MH

A large genus, mainly annual and perennial climbers, named after Karl Pehr Thunberg, a Swedish botanist and friend of Linnaeus. Only one species is much used as a houseplant, and even this would be better on a balcony or in a sunny porch for the summer than indoors.

How to grow
Easily raised as an annual, so there is little point in trying to overwinter the plant. If you do over-winter it, cut it back rigorously in late winter or early spring.

Thunbergia alata

Provide good light, keep the compost moist, and feed fortnightly.

The plant will need support if grown in a pot, but you could grow it in a hanging pot, where it will both cascade and climb up the hanging supports.

Propagation

Seed sown in spring. Pinch out the tips of young plants to encourage bushiness.

SOME POPULAR SPECIES	
T. alata (South Africa) A hairy climber with thin, heart-shaped, toothed leaves. Bright orange four-petalled flowers up to 4 cm (1½ in) across, with a dark centre.	Some hybrids have white or pale yellow flowers, both with and without the 'black eyes'.

Tillandsia

(flowering, non-scaly type)
PS/H/HH

There are two main types of these bromeliads: those with strap-like 'normal', green leaves, usually grown for their flowers, and the so-called air plants which have scaly, usually grey leaves that are grown more out of curiosity value than for their beauty.

The scaly, 'air plant' tillandsias are described on the next page.

How to grow

Use soft water. Mist regularly, and use a foliar feed occasionally when the plants are growing. Water sparingly in winter.

Little compost is needed, and they can be grown as epiphytes on a 'bromeliad tree'. If growing in compost, use three parts ericaceous mix to one part sharp sand.

Propagation

Detach rooted offsets from parent plants and pot up separately.

SOME POPULAR SPECIES	
T. flabellata (Mexico, Guatemala) Narrow, strap-like leaves, arising from base, about 25–50 cm (10–20 in) tall. Red bracts and blue flowers with protruding yellow stamens. **T. leiboldiana** (Mexico) Soft green, narrow leaves,	about 30 cm (1 ft) long. Flower spike with red bracts and blue flowers. **T. lindenii** (Peru) Narrow, linear leaves, crowned with flowers on a flattened spike composed of violet-pink bracts from which dark blue flowers emerge in succession.

Tillandsia lindenii

Tillandsia

(scaly type/air plants)
PS/W/MH

Tillandsia concolor

These are interesting rather than beautiful plants. Until relatively recently they were regarded as rather difficult, needing misting several times a day, and quite unsuitable for the home. Now they are widely sold, in Britain at least, as decorations for the home. Experience has now shown that even daily misting is not essential (though it is always worthwhile), and they are really tough plants. They are not, however, pot-plants. You can fix them to a branch with moss, or simply pop them in a decorative sea shell, or even fix them to your dressing-table mirror. Clearly they are houseplants with a difference.

How to grow
First arrange them attractively. Keep them in a reasonably light position, mist daily if possible, and add a liquid fertiliser to the water once a week in summer. They are able to absorb moisture from the air.

Propagation
Some species, such as *T. usneoides*, can be propagated by removing a few shoots and tying them together and attaching to a new support. Offsets may eventually be produced by other species and these can be detached.

SOME POPULAR SPECIES
With the exception of *T. usneoides*, these tillandsias form rosettes of greyish leaves similar to the one illustrated, *T. concolor*. **T. usneoides** (Tropical America) (Spanish moss) Unlike the other species, the Spanish moss hangs down in long cascades of almost root-like greyish leaves.

Tradescantia

Inch plant/Wandering Jew
PS/C/MH

The species used as pot-plants (there are also hardy border plants in the genus) have long been used in the home. Usually they are neglected and without a little care will cling tenaciously to an existence while lacking real appeal.

How to grow
These plants do not need a lot of water, but they will be far healthier if you prevent the compost drying out completely, even in winter.

Varieties of *Tradescantia*

Position and pinching are both important. A light position is necessary to maintain good variegation (but direct summer sunshine may scorch the leaves), and pinching is necessary to maintain a bushy shape and to stop the trailing stems becoming too thin and long. You will also need to pinch out shoots where the variegation is inferior, especially any all-green shoots.

Feed weekly from spring to autumn.

The plants will almost certainly deteriorate with time, so keep a supply of fresh plants coming along from cuttings (several plants in one pot will give a better, more even display).

Propagation
Cuttings root very easily, even in water.

SOME POPULAR SPECIES	
T. albiflora (South America) Creeping or trailing stems with stemless leaves about 4.5–6 cm (1¾–2½ in) long. The variegated forms are the ones cultivated, such as 'Albo-vittata' (cream stripes along leaves), 'Rochford Silver' (white stripes), and 'Tricolor' (white and pale purple stripes). **T. blossfeldiana** (Argentina)	A semi-erect species with 4–8 cm (1½–3 in) leaves dull green above, purple and hairy beneath, and usually fleshy purple stems. 'Variegata' has cream stripes. **T. fluminensis** (South America) Similar to *T. albiflora*, and grown in variegated forms such as 'Quicksilver'. In bright light the undersides of the leaves may turn pale purple.

Vriesea
PS/H/HH

A genus of about 200 bromeliads that are either terrestrial or epiphytic, native to Central and South America. The one most widely grown is *V. splendens*.

The vriesea that you buy will almost certainly consist of a single 'vase'. *V. splendens* is sometimes sold as seedlings in small pots, often unlabelled, which will take years to flower, so you will need patience. The plants die after flowering, but they should give you a couple of months of pleasure first.

How to grow
If you buy a plant in flower, simply avoid very hot, dry air, otherwise place it where it looks good.

Young plants not in flower will need a light position out of fierce sunshine. Water freely during the summer, give less in winter. Use soft water for this and for pouring into the 'vase'.

Keep the humidity high. Feed monthly from spring to autumn.

Use a potting compost of three parts ericaceous mix to one part sharp sand.

Propagation
Offsets will grow around the old stem, and these can be removed when large enough.

SOME POPULAR SPECIES	
V. saundersii (Brazil) Similar to *V. splendens* (which is better known) but shorter, with grey-green leaves usually lacking the bands or patches. The inflorescence is more open and drooping.	**V. splendens** (Guyana) (Flaming sword) Rosette of sword-shaped but arching green leaves with purple-brown cross-banding. The spear-like inflorescence with orange or red bracts stands above the rosette.

Vriesea splendens

Yucca
FS/C/MH–LH

Yuccas are among the best-selling houseplants, perhaps because they are so tough and seem to do well even in inexperienced hands.

How to grow
Good light will do the plants good, and they will grow in a sunny window that would be unsuitable for most other houseplants in high summer. They can also be stood outdoors for the summer, where they make interesting patio plants.

Water freely in summer, keep the compost drier in winter.

Repot each spring. A clay pot and loam-based compost will help to give the plant stability.

Propagation
Not normally a job for the amateur—even most of those grown commercially are imported (those sold in Europe may have been grown from stems imported from Honduras, for instance). You can, however, try rooting any sideshoots that appear.

SOME POPULAR SPECIES	
Y. aloifolia (Southern USA, West Indies) (Spanish bayonet) Spiky rosette of stiff, spine-tipped, sword-shaped leaves up to 50 cm (20 in) long. Often on a stout	trunk-like stem. **Y. elephantipes** (Central America) (Spineless yucca) Similar to the previous species, but without the sharp tips.

Yucca elephantipes

Zantedeschia
Arum lily, calla lily
PS/W/MH

A genus of about eight species that occur in partially marshy ground in parts of Africa and South Africa, with flowers borne on a spadix surrounded by a large spathe—the main feature of these plants. Zantedeschias can look nice in a pot, but they are not ideal houseplants.

Zantedeschia rehmannii

How to grow
If buying a dry rhizome, pot it up in the autumn and water freely. Keep the compost just moist, but water freely once shoots appear. After flowering (which is usually in spring), rest the plant by greatly reducing the amount of water for a month or two. Then repot and water normally to encourage it into growth again.

Propagation
Divide rhizomes when repotting.

SOME POPULAR SPECIES	
Z. aethiopica (South Africa) Deep green, arrow-head shaped leaves that die down when the plant is resting. White spathes about 15–23 cm (6–9 in) long which are long lasting if kept cool.	**Z. rehmannii** (Transvaal) (Pink arum) Similar to above but the leaves are sometimes flecked white, and the smaller spathes, about 8 cm (3 in) long, are usually tinged pink or purple along the edges, deeper purple inside.

Zebrina
Wandering Jew
PS/W/MH

Zebrinus means striped in Latin, and many of the species have striped leaves. In fact they closely resemble the variegated tradescantias much grown as houseplants.

How to grow
Provide a position in good light to maintain good colouring and variegation, but avoid direct summer sunlight.

Avoid overwatering and over-feeding, otherwise compactness and colour may suffer, but water moderately in summer. They will benefit from high humidity.

Repot each spring—several plants to a pot should make a better display than a single plant. Pinch them back if they become straggly and give the plants space to trail. They are good subjects for a suspended pot or a hanging basket.

Propagation
Cuttings root very easily.

SOME POPULAR SPECIES	
Z. pendula (Mexico) Creeping or trailing stems. Ovate leaves about 2.5– 7.5 cm (1–3 in) long, green with two silvery	bands on top, suffused purple below. The variety 'Quadricolor' is striped in green, white and purple and very decorative.

Zebrina pendula

Terms & Techniques

This section includes an explanation of technical and horticultural terms used in the first part of the book, as well as some that you might encounter in other houseplant books.

It is more than just a glossary, however. Where relevant, the practical implications are explained, and for practical tasks the jobs are illustrated with step by step illustrations.

We have not included specific chemicals for pest and disease control because these vary from country to country, and new ones are continually appearing, sometimes to replace current controls.

If you familiarise yourself with this part of the book you should find it a useful aid to propagation and houseplant care as well as a source of explanation for those terms and techniques that you may not be quite sure about.

Acid compost
A compost with a low pH (*see* pH), necessary for those plants affected by too much lime. *See* Chlorosis, Compost, and Ericaceous compost.

Aerial roots
Aerial roots grow from stems above compost or soil level, and can extract moisture from the air. They sometimes help the plant cling to a support.

Among the plants that produce aerial roots are many philodendrons, *Monstera deliciosa*, and some selaginellas.

Air layering
Few houseplants can be propagated by conventional layering, because it is not practical to peg down suitable stems. Air layering does not depend on the stem being brought into contact with the ground.

A couple of inches below a leafy part of the plant, make a slanting cut with a sharp knife, being careful not to slice through the stem. If you are worried by this, simply remove a strip of 'bark' about 1 cm (⅜ in) wide right round the stem. Dust or paint with a rooting hormone.

Tie a piece of polythene round the stem, securing above and below the moss. Black polythene will assist rooting but a transparent sheet may enable you to see roots developing. One solution is to use a second layer of black polythene, which you can remove to check on progress.

Pack damp sphagnum moss around the stem (you can use peat instead but you will have to put the polythene on first then pack in the peat).

Once roots have formed (it could take as little as a month or more than six months), sever the plant and pot it up.

The rooted top half can be potted up to form a new plant, while the old plant from which it has been severed will, in all probability, start growing again from one or two buds to produce another new plant.

Air plant

A group of bromeliads belonging to the *Tillandsia* genus, able to absorb moisture and nutrients from the air. They can therefore grow without soil (one of the most famous air plants—*T. usneoides*, Spanish moss, festoons telegraph wires in some parts of the world). They are not bright plants—grey is the usual colour—but make interesting indoor decorations. One is illustrated on page 98.

Not all tillandsias are air plants.

Annual

An annual is raised from seed, grows, flowers, and then dies, all within a season. This is usually within the same year, but some can also be sown late one year to flower early the next (like biennials).

Some houseplants are treated as annuals (capsicums, for instance) because although they may live for another year they are unlikely to be successful.

Aphids

A group of insects of which greenfly and blackfly are the most common. These attack a wide range of houseplants, and are likely to be the most frequent pests on your houseplants. Fortunately they are easily controlled by a wide range of insecticides.

Areole

Found on cacti. A small, hairy, cushion-like swelling, frequently bearing sharp spines and barbed hairs (known as glochids).

Aroid

A plant that belongs to the Araceae (arum) family. Most of those of commercial interest as houseplants come from the jungles of Central and South America (though some, such as *Aglaonema*, come from Asia or Africa). Most of them are climbers, and their aerial roots provide support as well as taking moisture from the humid atmosphere.

Aroids used as houseplants include aglaonema, caladium, dieffenbachia, monstera, philodendron, scindapsus, and syngonium.

Bottle garden

Collection of small, usually slow-growing plants in a large bottle—traditionally a carboy but now much more likely to be a purpose-made glass container, or green bottles made primarily for other purposes (to hold olives for instance).

Most of the ready-planted bottle gardens sold today are unsealed and merely a way of displaying a collection of plants for a relatively short period.

True bottle gardens are sealed (normally with a cork bung), and if the environment is properly balanced (with the right amount of moisture) the plants should live without watering or other attention for at least six months provided that the bottle is positioned in a light but not sunny place.

Use a funnel and tube to place layers of gravel, charcoal, and compost on the base without getting them all over the sides of the container.

You can use bamboo 'tweezers' or a fork tied to a cane to position the plants into holes that have already been made with a spoon fixed to a cane.

Use a cotton reel pushed on to a cane to tamp the compost around the plants, then use a syringe to moisten the compost and clean the glass. Or you can use a fine mist sprayer instead, but be careful not to make the compost too wet or you may have problems with the plants rotting off.

Botrytis

Popularly known as grey mould, this fungus disease can be a particular problem in cold, damp conditions. The fungus usually starts on dead or dying tissue (dead flowers or fallen leaves for instance), but if left unchecked can spread to affect healthy tissue. The common name of this disease is apt—the affected part becomes enveloped in a grey mound of fluffy mould. If moved or disturbed, dust-like spores may fly up and start new infections.

Many modern fungicides will control botrytis if you treat the plant early, but good hygiene (pick off dead or diseased leaves or flowers regularly), and avoiding a cool, damp atmosphere, will do much to prevent the problem.

Bract

A modified leaf, sometimes scale-like and green or brown, but sometimes bold and highly coloured, and possibly resembling a coloured leaf or flower. The popular poinsettia (*Euphorbia pulcherrima*) has large highly coloured leaf-shaped bracts; the aphelandra has a bract that forms a spike containing the less conspicuous true flowers.

Bracts can be much longer-lasting than flowers.

Bromeliad

A member of the Bromeliaceae (pineapple) family, of which there are about a thousand species. The plants are usually stemless, or short-stemmed, with stiff and usually spiny leaves.

Bromeliads are mainly epi-phytic (they grow on trees, not on the ground), and many of them have leaves arranged in a rosette that forms a water-retaining 'vase', from which the plant can derive moisture and nutrients. In many species this is kept topped up during the growing season.

Bromeliad tree

A method of displaying bromeliads. An old forked tree branch can be used, but it must be well anchored into a firm, perhaps concrete, base. Bromeliads are wired to the branches, or wedged into forks with sphagnum moss packed round the roots.

Bromeliads grown this way can look very decorative, but they will need regular misting to maintain a humid atmosphere (in a pot this would be less crucial). It is no use displaying a bromeliad tree in a dark corner, no matter how pretty it looks. The plants need adequate light.

Calyx

The outer, protective part of a flower, consisting of a ring of usually green modified leaves (the sepals) that are fused together at the base to form a bowl, funnel, or tube around the petals.

Capillary action

The means by which a liquid is drawn upwards through a confined space, such as the gaps between soil particles.

Chlorosis

The loss of, or lack of, chlorophyll (the green colouring matter in leaves) usually due to the lack of certain available elements in the compost necessary for its production. The leaves become bleached or yellow.

Plants that prefer an acid compost may become chlorotic if the compost contains too much lime, which prevents these plants from obtaining some essential nutrients.

Chlorotic plants outdoors can be treated with a chelated compound (Sequestrene), but for pot plants the solution is to use an acid compost (*see* Ericaceous compost). Always use soft water (*see* Water) for these plants.

Compost

The compost is crucially important for pot-grown plants. Earlier generations of gardeners used to have favourite recipes with ingredients that most of us would find practically impossible to obtain now: leaf-mould, quality fibrous loam, crushed bones, decomposed sheep manure, mortar rubble and crushed brick, and even crushed potsherds, are examples. Fortunately, most plants will grow well in one of the modern standard potting composts. But some will do better in one type than in another. Where there *is* a clear benefit from one type of compost—peat-based, loam-based, or a special acid mix, this has

been indicated in individual entries in the first part of the book.

Loam-based composts have a natural reservoir of nutrients lacking in peat-based composts, and they can 'hold' nutrients more easily. It is generally much easier to tell when loam composts need watering, and they are less likely to be a problem if they do dry out. For some plants the weight is an advantage if the plant has a lot of top growth that could make it top-heavy.

In Great Britain John Innes compost is the most widely used loam-based compost. This is a formula, not a particular brand. Apart from seed compost, there are three 'strengths' of potting compost: Nos. 1, 2 and 3. A higher number indicates a higher strength of fertilisers.

Peat-based composts are generally less variable in quality than loam-based composts, and they are light to carry home, and relatively 'clean' to use. Unfortunately they are easy to overwater, and difficult to rewet once they dry out. They will also run out of nutrients more quickly than loam composts, so feeding is much more important.

Both loam-based and peat-based composts contain lime to bring it to a suitable pH level for most plants. This may be all alkaline for some, in which case you should use an ericaceous mix (*see* Ericaceous compost).

Crocks

Crocks are most frequently mentioned in older books, when clay pots were the only ones available. Breakages meant plenty of pieces of broken pot that could be placed (concave side down) over the rather large drainage hole in another clay pot. This was called crocking.

The widespread use of plastic pots has made a supply of broken pots somewhat scarcer, and the smaller holes in plastic pots do not

need crocking in the same way anyway.

Clay pots still have a use, however (*see* Pots). If you need an alternative to cover the large drainage hole, try pieces of broken polystyrene tiles.

Crown

The basal part of a plant from which roots and shoots grow. Usually refers to the part of the rootstock just below or at soil level, from which the shoots grow (and to which they die back).

Cultivar

This is the botanist's name for a variety raised in cultivation. Some varieties of a plant occur naturally, and these are regarded as botanical varieties and should be printed in italics, with a lower case initial letter, after the species name. Most varieties occur in cultivation (sometimes by chance, often the result of a breeding programme), and these are strictly 'cultivars', which should be printed in Roman type, in single quotation marks, and with a capital initial letter.

To the gardener it makes no difference whether the variety occurred in a garden or in the wild (it makes the plant no more or less desirable), and to most gardeners 'variety' is more familiar and less pedantic so we have used that term throughout this book.

Cutting

There are many types of cutting (including leaf cuttings and leaf bud cuttings), and those applicable to houseplants are described under the relevant entry. The majority of cuttings, however, are stem cuttings. These should root easily and quickly if taken during the spring and summer months.

Most houseplant cuttings are taken from soft stems, and only on some shrubby plants should it be necessary to use older and harder stems.

Always choose healthy, vigorous shoots free of pests and diseases. Cut them off just below a node (joint where a leaf arises), and remove enough of the lower leaves to have a bare stem to insert in the compost.

Rooting hormones (there are liquids as well as powders) may speed rooting, but many plants will root without them. Some will even root in a jar of water and this is always worth trying if plenty of cutting material is available.

Use an all-purpose compost, or a seed compost (vermiculite and perlite are also very successful) for rooting cuttings; potting compost may contain a harmful level of nutrients.

A propagator will help to root the more difficult kinds, but most houseplants that can be raised from cuttings will root successfully on a light windowsill in a warm room. You will, however, need to provide the necessary humidity with the aid of a polythene bag, and avoid direct sunlight, which could overheat or scorch the plants.

Deciduous
The term means that the plant loses its leaves at the end of the growing season (in other words, it is not evergreen). But it is normally used in the context of trees and shrubby plants, rather than herbaceous plants.

Division
Division is a self-explanatory term—it is simply a matter of dividing the old plant.

Outdoors it may be necessary because the clump is becoming too large as much as for propagation. With houseplants, it is more normal to divide suitable plants as a means of multiplication.

Not all plants are suitable. Only those with a fibrous root system and a crown that can be divided into sections containing both shoots and roots will be successful propagated this way.

Many ferns can be propagated successfully by division, which is much quicker and easier than raising them from spores. Older plants of saintpaulias which have formed several crowns will also divide easily.

Remove the plant from its pot, shake off any loose soil and then gently pull the moist root-ball apart into small pieces. Sometimes the root-ball may have to be dissected with a sharp knife. Repot the divided sections into smaller pots.

Dormant period
A temporary period when the plant ceases to grow, usually but not always coinciding with winter. Some plants will not show this dormancy if the temperature is too high, but may suffer in the long term if they are not 'rested'.

Drawn
A term used to decribe a plant that has been 'drawn' towards the light, becoming weak, long-jointed, and probably pale in the process.

Epiphyte
A plant adapted to living above the soil, usually on tree branches (*epi* = upon, *phyton* = plant) or on mossy rocks. Bromeliads and orchids are typical epiphytes. The roots that cling to the surface of the branch or rock are not parasitic, although they may derive some nutrients from decaying plant

remains. They can derive moisture and nutrients from the air or decaying plants and insects.

Ericaceous compost

An acid compost containing very little or no lime. Ericaceous plants (those belonging to the Ericaceae or heather family) are generally lime-haters, but plants belonging to other families may also dislike lime in the compost.

You can buy both loam-based and peat-based ericaceous compost mixes, though they are less widely available than ordinary composts.

Evergreen

A plant that does not shed its leaves all at the same time, like a deciduous tree or shrub. Although the leaves are shed as new ones grow, this is done gradually so the plant always appears to be clothed.

Eye cutting

The 'eye' is an undeveloped or immature bud. In the case of an eye cutting, a section of stem is chosen that contains an undeveloped growing point in the axil of the leaf. The stem is cut up into sections, sometimes containing a leaf and leaf stalk, and these are inserted into the compost with the leaf above. Large leaves, such as those on *Ficus elastica*, are usually rolled up and secured with an elastic band to reduce water loss from the leaf.

Not many plants are propagated this way, and it is mainly of practical use to commercial growers.

Feeding

Most plants need feeding (*see* Fertilisers), but plants can be overfed, and the build-up of salts can become toxic. Other plants may grow too large or too rapidly if fed regularly. We have tried to give an indication of how much fertiliser a particular plant needs by giving a frequency (weekly, fortnightly, monthly). But this is only a guide to how 'hungry' those plants are, because how often you feed also depends on the type and strength of the fertiliser used.

Fertiliser

Most, but not all, plants will reward you with a much better display if you feed them (*see* Feeding).

The best type of fertiliser to use depends as much on your own discipline and interest in the plants, as on the merits of the actual brand or formulation used.

Liquid fertilisers (*and soluble powders*) are popular, but are most reliable if you are methodical and remember to apply them regularly.

The plants are unlikely to appreciate one brand much more than another if they receive the same amount. And to know how much you are giving them means that you have to study the small print and do some calculations (which few of us want to be bothered with).

There are, however, some general points to bear in mind. Some fertilisers are so weak that you can almost apply them at every watering to most plants, others are much more concentrated and therefore need applying less often.

Do not feel that you have to use a feed described as a 'houseplant' fertiliser. One for the garden is likely to be just as good and may be cheaper. But if it makes a gallon at a time and you only want a pint, it may be worth paying a premium for convenience.

Some liquids are applied as drops directly to the pot. At least you know how much you have given an in-

dividual plant, but you will have to water it in (and all fertilisers should be applied to compost that is already damp), so you will not save much effort.

Many liquid fertilisers can also be absorbed through the leaves (*see* Foliar feeding), but this is not normally necessary.

Fertiliser sticks and pellets that are pushed into the compost and release their nutrients slowly over a period of weeks or months are well worth thinking about if you find liquid feeding a chore. There are also slow-release fertilisers that you can incorporate into or sprinkle on the compost, though you may not like their appearance on the surface.

All these products will make the theory of feeding weekly, fortnightly, or monthly rather academic. The fertiliser is there for the plants to take as they need it. And you can hardly remove them as the resting period arrives—although this may not be a problem as many of them only release the nutrients when the temperature is warm enough for growth.

Plants can be over-fed. Too much fertiliser can cause toxicity problems, especially in sensitive plants.

Floret

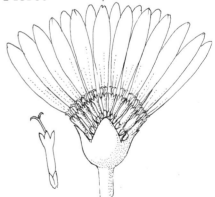

A single flower that forms part of a large head. In the daisy family (Compositae), each flower is really a head of tiny but closely-packed florets around a central disc.

Foliar feeding

Some fertilisers are sold specifically as foliar feeds, but many ordinary liquid (and soluble powder) fertilisers can also be used as a foliar feed (the plants absorb the nutrients through the leaves). Generally it will do just as much good down at the roots, but for plants such as the air plant tillandsias, which take their nutrients from the air, applying a weak dose of fertiliser in a mist over the foliage is both practical and necessary.

Frond

The feathery leaf of a fern or palm. Generally, but not always, much-divided and arching.

Fungicide

A chemical that will kill or control fungus diseases (or at least some of them). It is not easy to spray fungicides on houseplants indoors, but some have a systemic action (although it may not be as effective as spraying the leaves), and these might be worth considering.

Genus (plural genera)

A group of allied species. The genus is the first word of a plant name, and has a capital letter when written as part of a full name: in *Berberis darwinii*, *Berberis* is the genus, *darwinii* the species (*see* Species).

The genus is equivalent to a Surname, the species to the individual and unique member of the family. A genus may contain only one species, or it may contain more than a thousand. It depends on how closely botanists consider various plants are related.

Germination

The emergence of a new plant from a seed. *See* Seeds.

Glochid

A small slender barbed hair, found on an areole (*see* Areole), characteristic of many cacti.

Grey mould

A disease characterised by a grey, fluffy growth of a fungal mould (*see* Botrytis).

Growth inhibitor/ regulator

Although you are unlikely to be able to buy these in shops, they are widely used commercially.

Chemicals may be used to dwarf plants that would otherwise become leggy, such as *Hypoestes phyllostachya* (syn. *H. sanguinolenta*), or to make dwarfer and bushier plants, such as poinsettias and all-the-year-round chrysanthemums.

These chemicals will not do your plants any harm—they make them more attractive—but bear in mind that without them the same plant that you raise yourself may not be so attractive, or may not be as compact.

Half-hardy

Likely to be damaged by frost. This term is usually applied to bedding plants that will survive the summer outdoors but not the winter.

'Hard' water

Water containing a high proportion of lime. Harmful to plants that need relatively acid conditions. *See* Watering.

Hardy

Generally taken to mean a plant that will not be killed by frost. But there are degrees of hardiness, and the more severe the frost the greater the number of plants likely to be damaged or killed.

Honeydew

A sticky secretion left on leaves by insects such as aphids and whitefly. It can be a particular problem because an unsightly black mould often grows on this, and looks disfiguring.

The solution is simple—control the insects responsible.

Hormone rooting preparations

Hormone rooting powders or liquids can be useful for rooting the more difficult plants, but many houseplants will root readily without assistance.

The two chemicals most widely used are naphthyl acetic acid (NAA) and indole butyric acid (IBA). There is some evidence that IBA is more effective on a wider range of plants, but both are useful.

Humidifier

A piece of equipment that will maintain a high level of humidity. Water is usually released as a fine spray, but this type can be noisy in use.

Evaporators work on the principle of heating water to evaporate it. These are efficient and silent.

Humidity

Humidity is the amount of moisture in the atmosphere. It is expressed as a percentage of complete saturation, but the amount of moisture that the air will hold varies with temperature. The hotter the air, the more moisture it can contain. Because warm air needs more moisture to become saturated the problem is worse in summer and in centrally heated rooms (where it can be nearer a desert level of 20–30 per cent than the 70–90 per cent that many houseplants have in their nature jungles).

In the home it is very difficult to maintain humidity high enough for most houseplants, which can result in leaves turning brown or yellow and shrivelling. As a rule, plants with thin, papery leaves are more vulnerable than plants with thick, fleshy leaves. A dry atmosphere also encourages red spider mite.

By using a humidifier you may be able to maintain humidity at about 40–60 per cent, which should be acceptable to you and the plants.

Although it is best to try to increase overall humidity, misting individual plants will certainly help, provided you do it often enough.

Double-potting, packing moist peat between the pots may help, but you must be careful not to let water stand in the outer container. And to be a practical solution the outer container would have to be wide enough to encompass most of the leaves—not likely with a wide-spreading plant. It might be better to arrange a group of plants together in a large container.

Hybrid

Usually a plant derived from crossing two distinct species or (much less commonly) genera.

Sometimes a crossing within a species is also described as a hybrid. But unlike an ordinary cross resulting from normal cross-pollination, which might produce an ordinary variety (technically, cultivar), these hybrids are likely to be the result of crossing two pure 'lines' (in other words stable varieties that breed true). The resulting cross is called an F1 hybrid. An F1 hybrid normally shows increased vigour, and in general is better than the contributing parents. There are F1 hybrid houseplants, for instance achimenes, begonias, calceolarias, cyclamen, and some primulas.

Hydroculture

Also known as hydroponics. A method of growing plants without compost. Special fertilisers (known as ion exchange fertilisers) are used in the water (which should be tap water, to start the necessary chemical reaction). You can use your own containers and buy the expanded clay granules and fertiliser, but it is much better to buy a plant already growing in a hydroculture pot unless you have already gained some experience.

Hydroculture plants are ideal if you have to leave them unattended for days or even weeks at a time— the water will need topping up only infrequently, and a new dose of fertiliser will only be necessary every six months.

Many plants are very successful grown this way, but it is a more expensive method than growing conventionally in compost.

Converting your own plants is possible but not easy, and beyond the scope of this book.

Do not assume that because hydroculture plants grow in water, plants can normally be allowed to stand in wet compost—different types of roots are produced for hydroculture and there is a gap above the water for the roots to receive air. Waterlogged compost will soon kill your plants.

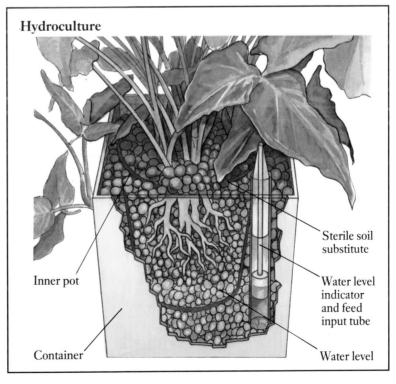

Hydroculture

Inner pot

Container

Sterile soil substitute

Water level indicator and feed input tube

Water level

Inflorescence

The part of a plant bearing flowers. It is a term often used not so much in its botanical sense but to describe a flower head or spike that is unlike a typical flower (perhaps a spike where colourful bracts are the main feature, with the true flowers of secondary importance).

Insecticide

A chemical for killing insects. Although there is a wide range of insecticides suitable for spraying on plants outdoors, you must be much more selective indoors.

First try to kill the pests with a fairly safe aerosol containing synthetic pyrethrum (the advantage of an aerosol is that you do not have to mix a large quantity of spray for say one or two plants, although it is an expensive way of buying insecticide).

You can also buy insecticidal 'pins' (small cardboard strips impregnated with a systemic insecticide) that are pushed into the compost.

If these methods fail to control a difficult pest, you may have to take your plant outside or into a greenhouse and use one of the more specific insecticides.

John Innes compost

In Great Britain, John Innes composts have been the standard loam-based composts for the last 30 years. John Innes is not a brand, but a formula, devised by the John Innes Institute.

Apart from a seed compost, there are three potting composts, Nos. 1, 2 and 3, containing increasing amounts of fertiliser. It is important to use the right one—too much fertiliser can inhibit growth, and in the case of seeds affect germination. *See* Composts.

John Innes composts may contain too much lime for plants that need an acid compost, but you may be able to buy a version with less lime (*see* Ericaceous compost).

Lanceolate

Term used to describe a lance-shaped leaf; one with a long, gradual taper.

Lateral shoot

Any shoot growing sideways from the main stem below the tip.

Layering

A method of propagation. One of the most popular forms of layering for houseplants is air layering (*see* Air layering), but simple soil layering is also possible with some climbers and trailers.

Although different methods of ground layering are used for outdoor plants, only one is really practical for indoor plants.

Take a flexible stem from a suitable plant and bend it down so that the stem is in contact with a pot of compost; you can hold it in position with a pebble, piece of bent wire, or even an old-fashioned clothes peg.

Layers often root more readily if the stem is injured, either by twisting, removing a small strip of tissue around the stem, or by making a small slit. However, all these treatments are much more difficult to do with a houseplant than with a tough shrub outdoors. If you do wound the plant, dust it with a hormone rooting powder.

Keep the compost moist, and sever the new plant from the parent once it has rooted satisfactorily. This may take many months however, and where there is a choice it may be better to take cuttings.

Plants that are suitable for layering indoors include hederas (ivies), and philodendrons.

See also Plantlets, and Offsets.

Layering

Leaf cutting

Leaf cuttings can be used to propagate a number of popular houseplants, including saintpaulias (African violets), sansevierias (mother-in-law's tongues), and some begonias.

Leaf petiole cuttings are used for plants such as saintpaulia, *Peperomia caperata*, and many begonias (but not *B. rex*).

Choose a new but fully expanded leaf and cut it off cleanly with a razor-blade or sharp knife, leaving about 5 cm (2 in) of the stalk attached to the leaf blade.

Make a hole in a pot or box of cuttings' compost just deep enough to take the stalk and hold the cutting with the blade resting on the surface. Angle the hole so that the leaf blade is almost flat on the compost when it is in position.

Firm the compost around the stalk, and water the cuttings with a fungicide before putting the pot in a propagator or covering it with a polythene bag. Keep the cuttings warm and in a light place but out of direct sunlight. Water sparingly until the cuttings have taken.

You will know that the cuttings have taken when new plantlets start to appear, growing up from compost level.

Midrib cuttings are used for plants such as gloxinias and streptocarpus, which have a single central vein. Choose a young, undamaged, but fully expanded leaf from a healthy plant.

Slice the leaf into strips not more than 5 cm (2 in) wide, so that each piece has a main vein in the centre and two flaps of leaf blade.

Insert the cuttings upright in a cuttings' compost, just deep enough to hold them erect. Spray with a fungicide, and treat as leaf petiole cuttings.

This method is also used for sansevierias, although the leaves do not have the central main vein like the others mentioned.

Leaf squares and *leaf slashing* can be used for *Begonia rex* and some related species.

Slashing simply involves turning the leaf over so that the main veins are on top, and cutting through the main veins with a sharp knife or razor-blade. Make the cuts about 2.5 cm (1 in) apart.

Place the slashed leaf on the surface of a cuttings' compost and peg down to keep the leaf blade in contact with the moist compost. Treat as petiole cuttings, but cover the seed tray or pot with a sheet of glass. Plantlets should form in about a month.

Alternatively you can cut the leaf up into pieces about 18 mm (¾ in) square and lay these on the surface of the compost, face up. Plants with wrinkled leaves will not lie flat in contact with the compost, and these will have to be inserted vertically into the compost.

Leaflet
A section of a compound leaf, usually resembling a leaf in itself.

Leaf mould
A confusing term. It has two meanings. It can be rotted leaves, an ingredient of some traditional potting compost mixtures; or a general term applied to various fungus diseases that rot leaves.

Most leaf-rotting diseases can be controlled to some extent by modern fungicides.

Leaf shine/gloss
If you want glossy-leaved plants to shine (the plant will be no better for it), either sponge down with soapy water (not detergent) or use a proprietary leaf shine. It is best not to apply these when the temperature is cold, or when the plant is exposed to direct sunlight. And it is always worth testing the product on a few leaves first before treating the whole plant—some plants are sensitive to some leaf shines.

Leaf spot
The name given to several fungal and bacterial diseases that cause brown or discoloured patches on leaves.

Leggy
A term used to describe a plant that has become drawn and spindly, usually because of lack of light. The stem becomes elongated between leaf joints, and the plant is generally weakened.

Light
In the home, plants are much more likely to suffer from lack of light than from lack of heat or moisture.

Few plants will thrive in a dark corner. Some, such as ferns and ivies, may serve to decorate it for a month or two but the chances are they will deteriorate steadily so you

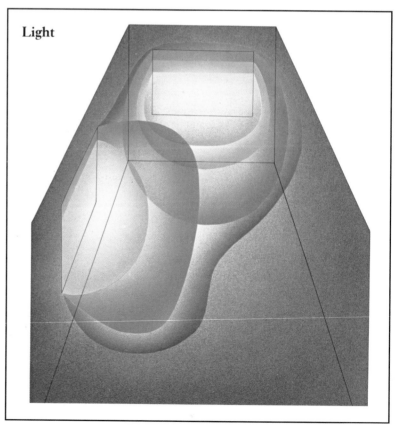

Light

need to be prepared to discard such plants after they have served their useful purpose.

Equally harmful for the vast majority of houseplants is intense sunshine. The sun's rays through the glass will scorch the leaves of most houseplants, resulting in dry, brown areas that look unsightly.

Although many of these plants enjoy sunshine outdoors, there the temperature is not intensified as it is behind glass, and the movement of air keeps the surface of the leaf cooler too. It is the excessive localised temperature that does the damage.

You will find that most of the entries in the first part of this book have a symbol indicating a requirement for good light but with protection from strong midday sun.

The ideal place for most houseplants is close to a window in an aspect that does not receive direct sun during the day. Also good are positions that receive only early-morning or evening sunshine. The alternative is to use screens such as blinds when the sun is most intense. Net curtains offer some protection.

The further from the window the plants are placed, the more they are likely to suffer. Light decreases in intensity as the square of the distance from the source. That means that if you move a plant twice as far into the room (say from 2 ft to 4 ft) it will receive only a quarter of the light.

Loam
In many ways, the 'ideal' soil: neither wet and sticky nor dry and sandy. A good blend of clay, silt, sand, and humus. Good loam has a fibrous texture.

Loam is a basic ingredient of traditional potting composts.

Loamless composts
Not all composts contain loam. Many are based on peat, but materials such as vermiculite may also be used. *See* Composts.

Long-day plants
These flower when the days are long and the nights short. They usually flower after they have been subjected to more than 12 hours of light each day for a period.

Mealy bug

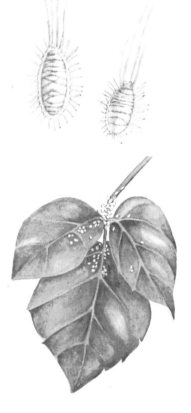

Easily identified pests. The young bugs are protected with what looks like a piece of cotton-wool. If only a few are present, pick them off or touch them with a paintbrush dipped in spirit. Otherwise use a systemic insecticide or spray (outdoors) with malathion.

Microclimate
The environment directly around the plant. Sometimes it is possible to produce a microclimate that is more conducive to growth than in the room generally—perhaps by misting or supplying extra warmth

or humidity. Grouping plants together also helps to produce a better microclimate and is very beneficial.

Micropropagation
A scientific method of propagation, usually using a very tiny portion of the growing tip (though there are several techniques) and growing these on using nutrient gels in sterile conditions to provide a supply of plants. Sometimes micropropagation is used to provide a large number of plants commercially, sometimes as a method of obtaining a supply of healthy virus-free stock.

It is possible to buy the equipment and nutrients to carry out the technique at home, but unnecessary unless you want to try it for fun.

Midrib
The main rib that divides a leaf centrally along the length. It usually stands out more prominently on the back of the leaf than other veins and ribs.

Mildew

A white, powdery deposit on the leaves, sometimes spreading to the stem too. Some plants are more susceptible than others (it can be a particular problem with begonias for example).

Pick off affected parts as soon as noticed. If the attack is severe it may respond to some of the modern fungicides, but the sooner an attack is treated the better the chances of success.

Mist

Misting a plant is a way of increasing humidity. It can be very successful *if done often enough*—even once a day may not be enough as the effect is fairly transient.

Use a fine mist, use soft water if possible (hard water can leave deposits on the leaves), and do not spray plants with hairy leaves.

Moisture meter

Moisture meters have a probe that you push into the compost. It will give you an indication of how moist the compost is, and often the meter comes with a list of preferred moisture levels for different plants.

These meters may be a help if you are a beginner, while you are learning how to judge by sight and feel. They are no substitute for good judgement—time of year, even type of day, should affect how when and how much you water.

Node

A point on the stem from which leaves arise. In the axils of the leaves are buds from which new shoots can develop.

The space between nodes (leaf joints) is known as the internode.

Offset

A young plant that appears naturally on the parent plant. There are various types: bulbs produce offsets as the parent bulb splits; some plants, such as houseleeks (sempervivums) produce small plants on short lateral stems.

Bromeliads produce offsets (new shoots arising from the base) before the parent plant dies.

Ovate

Egg-shaped in outline, broadest at the base.

Palmate

A compound leaf shape, with lobes radiating like the fingers of a hand.

Peat compost

Peat-based composts have become very popular in recent years. They can be produced to a consistent standard, and are light and not unpleasant to handle.

Lime is added to bring the pH up to an acceptable level, and nutrients to support plant growth. Sand or other ingredients may be used to produce a suitable structure and texture.

Perennial

A plant that lives for more than two years. Some plants that are perennial in the wild may be treated as annuals in cultivation.

Petiole

Leaf stalk.

pH

A scale by which the acidity or alkalinity of the soil or compost is measured. The scale runs from 0 to 14, though the extremes are never encountered in horticulture. Although 7 is technically neutral, 6.5 can be regarded as neutral horticulturally, most plants will grow at this level. Most houseplants will tolerate a relatively wide pH range, but where particular ones need an acid compost this has been indicated in the relevant entry.

Phototropism

There is a propensity for plants to grow towards light, which can be a particular problem in the home, where light is usually from one direction—the window.

Plants show varying degrees of phototropism, but with some the 'best' side of the plant may be facing out of the window and away from the room. Turning the plant a quarter of a turn each day may help to overcome this. But be careful about turning plants in flower or bud. Some, such as azaleas, clivias, gardenias, and the Christmas and Easter cacti, will drop buds or flowers if turned at a critical stage.

Pinching out

This is a form of pruning to encourage the plants to branch out. By removing the growing tip, shoots below are encouraged to branch out to take over. It is a technique usually used for plants that would otherwise tend to become leggy.

Pinna (plural pinnae)

The individual leaflet of a deeply divided leaf, such as a fern frond.

Plantlet

A small plant that may appear on the parent—sometimes on or around the leaf (*see* Tolmiea and Kalanchoe). Chlorophytum produces plantlets on runners.

Pot-bound

A term used to indicate the stage at which the pot has become so full of roots that growth of the plant is suffering. Most plants need repotting once the compost appears full of roots, but a few actually thrive in a cramped pot—sansevierias for instance.

Pots

Pots now come in many shapes and sizes—including square—not to mention colours.

Most pots nowadays are plastic, and for many plants these are perfectly suitable. The compost is less likely to dry out so quickly, and they wipe clean easily so unsightly deposits are unusual.

Be cautious of colours—some will be affected by strong sunlight. Square pots are easier to pack into a small space, but this is more likely to be more important in a greenhouse than the home.

Do not dismiss clay pots. They will make overwatering less likely, can look more 'right' for some plants, and for plants with large or heavy top growth palms, sansevierias, yuccas, for instance, the extra weight might be a useful counterbalance.

Sometimes a normal pot is too deep for the size of plant or the amount of root growth. Half pots (roughly half the depth of a normal pot) are better for many cacti and bromeliads for instance.

Potting on

Moving a plant on into a pot of a larger size, usually one or two sizes up. Never pot on into a pot much larger than the present size, otherwise the compost may become either exhausted or 'sour' before the plant has a chance to use it.

Potting on

1. Turn upsidedown and rap pot rim to loosen plant.

2. Place some compost in the base of the new pot, position the plant and trickle compost around the rootball, firming as the space is filled in.

3. Give the plant a gentle tap on a hard surface to help to settle the compost.

4. Sprinkle some more compost over the surface to fill any remaining gaps and water well.

Pot up

Move a seedling or rooted cutting into a pot for the first time.

Pricking out

A term used to describe the job of lifting individual seedlings from the box or pot in which they were sown and planting them into individual pots or spacing them out in a box.

Propagation

Act of raising new plants by seed or vegetative means (cuttings, layering, for instance).

Propagator

Cabinet for germinating seeds, raising seedlings, or rooting cuttings. Most are heated to provide the necessary warmth, and enclosed to maintain humidity.

Remember that a propagator must be placed in good light (though certain seeds may germinate better in darkness, the seedlings will need a light position). Avoid direct sunlight, however, as this may increase the temperature too much and cause scorching.

Red spider mite

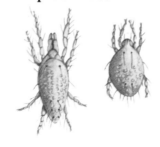

These are tiny insects difficult to notice until the population has become large. The young are flesh coloured, the adults reddish-brown. Webs may be formed between the leaves and stems. Leaves may become mottled and yellow.

Try immersing the top growth in an insecticidal solution. Difficult to eradicate once they have an established hold. Increasing the humidity around the plant helps to prevent this problem.

Repotting

The term repotting is loosely used to mean putting the plant into a new pot, whether the same size or larger. More specifically it means replanting in the same sized pot after removing some of the old compost and replacing with new. Moving the plant on to a larger pot is more correctly 'potting on'.

Rest/resting period

Many plants have a natural resting period, when they are either dormant or making little or no new growth. This is not necessarily accompanied by a loss of foliage.

Rhizome

A creeping, usually swollen, horizontal stem, growing either underground or on the surface. A storage organ.

Root-ball

The mass of roots and compost when a plant is removed from its pot.

Rosette

An arrangement of clustered leaves radiating from a central area.

Runner

A long shoot sent out by some plants, that will root and form new plants where it comes into contact with the soil.

Scale

Scale insects look like small yellowish-brown insects that resemble small scales or shells.

Seeds, plants from
Although many houseplants can be raised from seed, and are commercially, in the home you are more restricted. If you have a greenhouse the possibilities are much better.

Then cover with a piece of glass and sheet of paper if you do not have a propagator.

Unless you know that the seeds need light to germinate, the airing cupboard is usually a warm place if you do not have a propagator—but be sure to bring the pot or tray out as soon as the first seedlings germinate.

They are immobile. You can wipe them off with a sponge soaked with an insecticide (but use waterproof gloves) or use a systemic insecticide.

Scorch
Glass can intensify sunshine and heat the plant tissue locally so that the leaf becomes scorched—leaving brown, papery, patches.

Because only a few plants are likely to be needed, sow the seeds thinly in a pot or half-pot of seed compost. Or space them out well in a seed tray prepared as shown.

Cover with about the seed's own depth of compost, place the pot in a bowl of water to let the moisture soak up from beneath, or water the seed tray.

Prick the plants off into individual pots or another seed tray, and keep in a very light position, turning regularly.

Short-day plants
Plants that flower as the nights become longer and the days shorter. They do not normally flower unless it is daylight for less than 12 hours for a period of time.

'Soft' water
Water containing little lime. *See* Watering.

Spadix

A fleshy spike which carries small flowers embedded in little pits in its surface. Usually surrounded by a spathe.

Spathe
A large bract, often brightly coloured, acting as a protective sheath round a spadix.

Species
An individual member of a genus. *See* Genus.

Spore
A minute 'seed', composed of a single cell, by which a plant such as a fern, moss, or fungus, can reproduce itself. The spores do not germinate and grow immediately into a plant resembling the parent, but produce an intermediate generation which carries the sex organs.

Ferns are difficult to grow from spores, and indoors it is really a task for the experienced.

Stamen
Male reproductive organ, which forms and carries the pollen.

Stop/stopping
To 'stop' a plant is to pinch out the growing tip to encourage lateral growths to develop. *See* Pinching out.

Strike
To root a cutting.

Succulent
A plant having fleshy stems and/or leaves able to store moisture so that it can withstand very dry conditions.

Systemic
A term used to describe insecticides and fungicides that can be taken up by the plant and translocated (moved about) within the plant. The chemical is taken up by the roots and will find its way to the leaves.

Tendril
A thread-like modified leaf or stem that can twine round a support to enable the plant to cling and climb.

Terrarium
A glass case or container used for growing and displaying plants. Sometimes sealed to create a 're-cycled' atmosphere.

Terrestrial
Growing on the ground (as opposed to an epiphyte or an aquatic plant). Usually only used to describe species that might also be epiphytes, such as orchids or bromeliads.

Tuber
A thickened fleshy root (as in a dahlia) or a fleshy underground stem (such as a potato). These are storage organs that help the plant in time of drought, and also help them to overwinter.

Water/watering
Overwatering probably kills far more plants than underwatering, but ill health and a slow death can also come from unsuitable water.

Tap water is perfectly all right for the majority of houseplants, but the lime in some 'hard' tap water can adversely affect plants that need an acid compost.

Where relevant this has been explained in the first part of the book, when 'soft' water has been advocated for plants that are likely to be vulnerable.

The problem is obtaining soft water if you live in a hard-water area—collecting rainwater is one of those jobs more often written about than done. It is not really a very practical solution.

Some water softeners (those that use kitchen salt) will not produce suitable water, but those that use a demineralisation process can be used. Failing that, boiled water can be used (allow it to cool and stand for a day), or even thawed ice-cubes if mixed with some ordinary water (make sure that the plants are not watered with chilled water!).

Whitefly

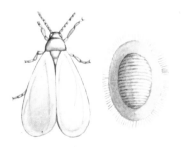

Tiny insects like small white moths, triangular in outline. They tend to fly up in a white cloud if the plant is disturbed.

Use a suitable insecticide, preferably as an aerosol or in systemic form.

Common Name Index

The most important Latin synonyms are also included

Picture credits
Bernard Alfieri: 19(t)
P. Ayers: 54(b)
Steve Bicknell: 8(t), 12(b), 19(b), 20(b), 28(t), 30(b), 47, 48(t), 49, 53, 57, 59, 64(b), 67(t), 72(t), 74(b), 93, 94(b), 101
P. Booth: 61
Michael Boys: 22(t)
Pat Brindley: 2, 33
R.J. Corbin: 106(l), 114(bl)
Eric Crichton: 46(t)
Alan Duns: 20(t), 34(b)
The Exotic Collection: 24(t)
Paul Forrester: 11(b), 14(t), 23(t), 38(t), 71, 74(t), 77(t), 78(b), 83, 95, 118

P. Hunt: 12(t)
A.J. Huxley: 92(t)
Naru Inui: 109(t)
Leslie Johns: 70(b)
Peter McHoy: 22(b), 90, 91(b), 98(t), 104, 106(r), 108, 111, 112(l), 114(t)
Bill McLaughlin: 5
Elsa Megson: 31
John Melville: 7(t,b), 8(b), 9, 10, 11(t), 13, 14(b), 16, 17(t,b), 18(t,b), 21, 23(b), 24(b), 25(t), 26(t,b), 27, 28(b), 29, 30, 32(t,b), 35, 36(b), 37, 38(b), 39, 40(b), 41, 42(t), 43, 46(b), 50(b), 51(t), 56(b), 58(b), 60(b), 63(t,b), 64(t), 65, 66, 67(b), 68(b), 69, 73, 76, 77(b), 78(t), 79, 82(t), 84, 85(b), 86,

88(t), 89, 91(t), 96(t), 98(b), 99, 100
P. Rosenwald: 40(t)
Harry Smith Horticultural Photographic Collection: 6, 34(t), 36(t), 42(b), 44(t), 45, 48(b), 56(t), 58(t), 62(b), 68(t), 72(b), 75, 82(b), 85(t), 87(t,b), 88(b), 92(b), 94(t), 96(b), 97, 100(b)
Peter Stiles: 70(t)
Pamla Toler: 25(b)
Jerry Tubby: 81(t)
Colin Watmough: 50(t), 62(t), 80, 81(b)
Michael Warren: 15, 44(b), 51(b), 52(t,b), 60(t)

Acknowledgements
The Publishers would like to thank the Challis Garden Centre, Boroughbridge Road, Poppleton, York, for their help in providing specimen plants for photography.